THE
COMPLETE
GUIDE TO
AMERICAN
KARATE &
TAE KWON DO

KEITH D. YATES

President of the American Karate and
Tae Kwon Do Organization (A-KaTo)

Forewords by Jhoon Rhee
and Chuck Norris

BLUE SNAKE BOOKS
Berkeley, California

Published by Blue Snake Books

Blue Snake Books' publications are distributed by
North Atlantic Books
P.O. Box 12327
Berkeley, California 94712

Cover and text design by Brad Greene
Printed in the United States of America

The Complete Guide to American Karate and Tae Kwon Do is sponsored by the Society for the Study of Native Arts and Sciences, a nonprofit educational corporation whose goals are to develop an educational and cross-cultural perspective linking various scientific, social, and artistic fields; to nurture a holistic view of arts, sciences, humanities, and healing; and to publish and distribute literature on the relationship of mind, body, and nature.

Blue Snake Books publications are available through most bookstores. For further information, call 800-733-3000 or visit our websites at www.northatlanticbooks.com or www.bluesnakebooks.com.

PLEASE NOTE: The creators and publishers of this book disclaim any liabilities for loss in connection with following any of the practices, exercises, and advice contained herein. To reduce the chance of injury or any other harm, the reader should consult a professional before undertaking this or any other martial arts, movement, meditative arts, health, or exercise program. The instructions and advice printed in this book are not in any way intended as a substitute for medical, mental, or emotional counseling with a licensed physician or healthcare provider.

Library of Congress Cataloging-in-Publication Data

Yates, Keith D.
  The complete guide to American karate & tae kwon do / by Keith D. Yates.
     p. cm.
  Summary: "Covers the development of the arts of karate and tae kwon do in the United States"—Provided by publisher.
  ISBN 978-1-58394-215-4
  1. Karate—United States. 2. Tae kwon do—United States. I. Title.
  GV1114.3.Y372 2008
  796.815'3—dc22

2007049286
CIP

1 2 3 4 5 6 7 8 9 SHERIDAN 14 13 12 11 10 09 08

Acknowledgments

The author extends his thanks to the following people who have provided instruction and inspiration:

Allen R. Steen

Skipper Mullins

J. Pat Burleson

Jhoon G. Rhee

James B. Toney

Bill Sosa

Ted Gambordella

Jon Baughman

Garrett Seaback

Michael Proctor

Jhoon Rhee, Keith Yates, and Chuck Norris

Contents

THREE Procedures 59

FOUR Physical Aspects 81

PROFILES

Foreword by Jhoon Rhee

Permit me to share a touching story I heard from Korean congressman Myung-Hwan Park, who was the chairman of the Foreign Affairs Committee of the Korean National Assembly from 1998 to 2002.

During the Japanese occupation of Korea in 1943, Mr. Hak-Yaul Kim was a high school boy in eleventh grade. He was forced into the Japanese Army a few years after World War II broke out, and was assigned to an army infantry company on the island of Saipan. There was one other Korean in his infantry unit. In the middle of bloody battle, the fellow Korean soldier fell sick with cholera.

In that war, if a soldier had a contagious disease, it was common to leave him to die for the safety of the other soldiers. Cholera is so dangerous that no one dares to come near the poor victim. But Mr. Kim carried the soldier everywhere and took care of him, supplying him with boiled water and doing the best he could to help him until, miraculously, he recovered.

After the war the men went their separate ways.

Then the Korean War broke out on June 25, 1950. Many Seoul residents were caught by surprise by an attack from the North, and the North Korean army captured many young South Koreans. Mr. Kim, now a government official, was among them. Officials were specific targets of the North Koreans, and as the solders searched his pockets, Mr. Kim realized that he had forgotten to get rid of his government ID card.

So he was sent off to be executed.

In middle of the night, a North Korean officer with a rifle slung over his shoulder came to where Mr. Kim was being held, awaiting execution. He called loudly, "Hak-Yaul Kim!"

"Yes, sir," Mr. Kim replied.

"You come with me," commanded the officer, and he took him out of the warehouse to a darkened cornfield.

Mr. Kim was sure that he was going to die that night. The officer took Mr. Kim to a quiet place and asked, "Did you fight in World War II?"

"Yes, sir," he replied.

The officer asked, "Did you help a Korean soldier who had cholera?"

"Yes, sir," Mr. Kim replied.

Then the officer said, "I was that soldier. You saved my life, then. It is my turn to save your life, Mr. Kim."

Shocked and relieved, Mr. Kim could not believe it was real, as the officer showed him the way to escape back to South Korea. Mr. Kim later became the Deputy Prime Minister of Korea.

The moral I wish to share with you is that you never know whom you are helping or harming in your everyday life. So it is wise to live with genuine love and compassion for people. Martial arts have taught me this and so many other lessons.

My life is the martial arts, and it is the same for Keith D. Yates. I have enjoyed Master Yates's writing over the years and consider him one of the best historians on the subject of tae kwon do and karate in America. This book shows his knowledge and understanding of more than just the technical aspects, but also the philosophy and the implications of a lifetime of martial study.

—Jhoon Rhee, the "Father of American Tae Kwon Do"

Martial arts have evolved tremendously over the last fifty years, with the modern forms largely originating from China, Okinawa, Korea, Japan, and Brazil. Great fighters have fine-tuned and mastered the techniques developed in each of these countries.

I easily get nostalgic thinking about the competitive champs of yesteryear, men like Allen Steen, Skipper Mullins, Roy Kurban, Benny Urquidez, Mike Stone, Joe Lewis, and Bill Wallace. I will always treasure the fights and the fellowship I had with many of these vintage combat warriors.

"What about Bruce Lee?" you may ask. Bruce was very fast, and he learned from everybody. He never believed in practicing only one style of martial arts, or that one style was the best. He said that everything had strengths and weaknesses, and what he wanted to do was find the strengths in each. He had a very open mind, and constantly learned from others.

When I first started working out with Bruce, he focused on kicking below the waist from his training in Wing Chun. I told him not to limit himself and to at least develop the ability to kick high, whether he used it or not.

I started to do my spinning heel kicks and hitting the pads. Then Bruce started doing it, and in six months he could do it as well as anybody. He worked out with me, Joe Lewis, and Mike Stone—he learned from all of us, as we learned from him. And in doing so, he added to his repertoire of techniques, as we did. Bruce Lee was far ahead of everybody else in that field. He had a vision that was years ahead of everyone. In one sense, although he was Chinese, he was the original American stylist.

In a recent poll by *Parade* magazine, Bruce Lee and I were named as the toughest martial arts movie stars ever. But I remind you that movies are quite different than real life. I love competition, but the more I study the Bible, the more I realize that beating someone is no way to feel fulfilled in life. Gratification at another's expense is not a commendable trait, but building up others at our own expense is.

Some might question my efforts to teach martial arts to young people by calling them a form of violence, but actually the martial arts are just the opposite. The bullies in this life are the ones who are afraid and do all the fighting, not those who develop a sense of worth and security by learning self-defense. When we assist these youngsters in maturing, developing self-esteem and respect for others—and then, all of a sudden, they realize they have no reason to fight—it's the most gratifying feeling in the world.

It isn't being the greatest champion but the greatest servant that ultimately matters. I know that might seem easy for me to say, having been a six-time world champion, but I mean it. It took me too many years to realize that it isn't the ladders we climb but the service we offer in this life that truly makes us great.

I am grateful for Keith Yates's service to the martial arts in so many ways. He is on our KickStart Advisory Board and has made a difference in many lives over the decades that he has taught and mentored thousands of students. I congratulate him on this book, just one more achievement in a lifetime of dedication to the martial arts.

—Chuck Norris, world champion and television and film star

Introduction

The American systems of karate and tae kwon do came into their own during the late 1960s.[1] The martial arts had been in this country for barely a dozen years when Americans began to turn them into a unique blend of traditions, practical self-defense, and modern sport. American karate and American tae kwon do really aren't so much styles of martial arts as much as ways of approaching the martial arts.

Americans, with their fascination with spectator sports like baseball, football, and boxing, wanted to make karate and tae kwon do into the next big national athletic attractions in the 1970s. Unfortunately, or maybe fortunately, that never happened, in spite of the explosion of tournaments on the American karate scene in those days. In retrospect that failure was actually good for the martial arts, because it forced many instructors to abandon the pursuit of tournament "glory" and to come back to the more beneficial themes of self-defense, physical fitness, and character building.

This book is meant to be a comprehensive reference to the American methods of karate and tae kwon do. Because every martial artist should know something about the history of his or her art, I have included interesting historical facts from both the Asian beginnings of these martial arts and their development in the United States. You'll also learn something about martial philosophy and about how you can integrate it into your everyday life. And, of course, we'll cover the many physical aspects of karate and tae kwon do, including basic techniques, sparring strategies, and self-defense. Interspersed throughout this book

you will find profiles of important American martial artists: men and women who have made the American styles into some of the most famous and perhaps even the best systems of martial arts in the world.

Right up front I want to mention something about the difference between karate and tae kwon do. As many American stylists practice them, there isn't much of a difference. As you will discover in the first chapter, many of the Korean nationals who came to the United States in the 1950s and 1960s used the term "karate" in reference to their martial art. Naturally the Japanese nationals also used this Japanese word. As a result, karate has become a generic term indicating any type of striking martial art. That is why many American tae kwon do stylists, myself included, use the terms karate and tae kwon do interchangeably. You still see Koreans, even today, putting the word "karate" on the windows of their tae kwon do schools.

Actually, you will find the greatest difference between styles in the United States a matter of whether they are "traditional" or "modern." In this book I will use "traditional" to describe karate and tae kwon do that put the emphasis on self-defense and character-building aspects like discipline and respect. "Modern" or sport karate and tae kwon do place a much higher emphasis on tournaments and competition techniques. Of course, that is not to say that traditional schools never enter tournaments or that schools with a bunch of trophies in the window don't teach character building, but you should check out the priorities of any school at which you want to train and decide which is best for you.

The American Karate and Tae Kwon Do Organization is a "traditional" organization featuring by and large "Americanized" schools. We strongly believe in teaching the lifetime benefits of the martial arts while incorporating elements from several disciplines that our instructors have found to be effective.

As you can see in the table of contents, this book includes history, philosophy, and some martial arts techniques. I have not included training patterns from all the many different systems of karate and tae kwon do, simply because there wasn't room. However, I have included five kata, three from tae kwon do and two from karate. Many of you probably use these forms and will find the diagrams a helpful reference.

Keith D. Yates

This has been a big undertaking, and I hope you'll have as much fun reading this book as I had writing it.

How to Pick a School

1. Ask about the school's emphasis, i.e., is it focused on self-defense or competition? If you want to learn self-defense, don't go to a school that piles everyone into a bus and travels to tournaments every weekend.

2. Watch a class to see if the instructors are good communicators and if the students respond positively to them. This is much more important than the number of stripes on the teacher's black belt. Some instructors are like a wise mentor, and others are like a drill sergeant.

3. Ask students and parents about their satisfaction levels. You may have to catch them in the parking lot after class, so they won't be speaking in front of the school owner.

4. Is the place clean, or is it badly in need of some fresh paint or a few air fresheners?

5. Does the school have an emergency first-aid kit, and is the instructor or office manager trained in how to use it? You might even ask about the last time someone got hurt in class.

6. Compare prices, yes, but cost is actually less of a factor than location. If the school is close, you'll probably attend more often.

7. If the school guarantees a black belt for a set (usually exorbitant) fee, find another school.

8. Speaking of fees, are there extra costs involved? Most schools do have testing fees, sign-up fees, etc., but they should all be explained up front. Incidentally, if there is a large sign-up fee ($200 or more), then the school probably doesn't expect its students to stick around for a long time.

9. Things that are important: how long the instructor has been teaching; being able to try out a few classes before having to pay a larger amount; the instructor-to-student ratio.

10. Things that are not important: the "style" of karate or tae kwon do that is taught; trophies in the window; whether or not the instructor is a "master" or is in a "hall of fame."

For more hints, go to www.akato.org.

Q&A about American Karate and Tae Kwon Do

How long will it take to learn to defend myself with karate or tae kwon do?

That depends on a lot of factors, but don't think signing up for a three-week class is going to do anything other than make you aware of some of the introductory principles. You'll have to practice your techniques consistently for several months. If you pay attention in class and practice on your own, you should learn the basics of self-defense in six months or so. To be really confident in your abilities, however, you would need to learn and train on a continuing basis.

Will training help me lose weight?

Maybe. The experts say that physical fitness is made up of three areas: cardiovascular endurance, muscular strength, and flexibility (see chapter four). Because we work on all three in a karate class, you will definitely become more "fit." Whether that translates to losing pounds and inches depends more on changing lifestyle habits like diet and daily exercise. Most people are more motivated to change these things when they begin karate training.

Will I learn Buddhism and have to meditate?

I'll answer that last part first. No, you will probably not do meditation (although some schools do breathing exercises). Most American instructors don't delve into the quasi-religious aspects of the martial arts (see chapter two). And truth be told, karate and tae kwon do are the least "spiritual" of the martial arts. Famous historian Donn Draeger has said the linking of karate to Buddhism is a late innovation and cannot be associated with either Okinawan or Japanese styles.[2] Tae kwon do is even more recent and was formulated from a mainly secular approach. Still, if you are concerned about it, talk to your prospective teacher.

Will I have to break boards and bricks?

At the more advanced ranks, most schools do have students break boards. I don't have mine try it until about six months or more, and even then we start out with a single pine board. Children's bones, by the way, are softer than adults' bones, so kids should only try breaking boards under a competent instructor's guidance. Bricks and concrete are much more difficult and shouldn't be tried by anyone except advanced students.

Will I get hurt?

Martial arts training has been proven to be less dangerous than most other contact sports like football, hockey, and even soccer. Careful instruction and the addition of foam rubber padding for competitors have greatly reduced the likelihood of injury for participants. Still, you are learning how to kick and punch at another person, so the risk, however minimal, is there. In my experience, the most common injuries include getting kicked in the shins and overstretched muscles.

Can you kill someone from a distance without touching him?

Sure, with a bow and arrow or a gun!

Is there really a "delayed death touch"?

The vast majority of martial artists I know say the "delayed death touch" is a myth. Also, there isn't much self-defense application to a technique that takes longer than a few seconds to work because your attacker isn't going to wait around a few hours or days for it to take effect.

Aren't martial arts just for kids?

Although you see lots of children in a typical class these days, there are still plenty of adults (even a few with gray hair). Remember that martial arts were originally designed for adults and have had to be reworked in much of their approach for kids. And of the benefits of karate usually touted for kids—increased ability to focus, improved self-confidence, a greater respect for others—all apply equally to adult practitioners.

My kid is sort of aggressive already. Will this make him a bully?

If you have a good instructor who stresses the aspects of humility and self-control, it should counteract his aggressive tendencies. Often bullies actually have low self-esteem, and because martial arts are famous for building up self-esteem, they grow out of their need to bully others to feel better.

Should I take tae kwon do or karate from a tournament champion?

I've found that the fact that an individual can score points in a competition has little relationship to her ability to communicate to students. In some cases, it may even mean she will be practicing for her next big tournament with you as a sparring partner! You simply want to find the best and most knowledgeable instructor for yourself.

How long will it take to get a black belt?

That varies from school to school. Generally speaking, it should take three to four years or more of constant practice. The "black belt clubs" in some commercial schools are fine ways to offer a few extra perks as long as they are not guaranteeing you a black belt in a couple of years or so.

Are all black belts the same?

Unfortunately, no. Some schools promote people to black belt after a brief two years and a final ten-minute examination. Other schools might require six to eight years of austere training culminating in a three-day test of endurance to earn the black belt. To further complicate things, there is no single governing body for certification of martial arts black belts in this country (or even in Asia for that matter).[3] While there are some large organizations, the average student has a hard time figuring out who is legitimate (see chapter three).

Do black belts have to register their hands as "lethal" weapons?

I remember seeing this on an old episode of *The Dick Van Dyke Show* (yes, I go back that far), in which Dick warns a bully that his hands are registered as "lethal" weapons. I don't know if that is where this myth started, but there are no current laws in any state that require a black belt to be registered.

Which is the best style?

Almost all legitimate styles have good things to teach. According to a famous martial arts axiom, the style doesn't make the man—the man makes the style. In other words, a good instructor is going to be able to teach you good martial arts no matter what the style. Also, Americans tend to blend techniques and approaches, so styles are even less important here than they might be in Asia. That being said, however, you still might want to educate yourself about the differences between "traditional" and "modern" styles or "hard" and "soft" styles (see chapter two).

ONE

History

It will take your entire life to learn karate; there is no limit.
—Gichin Funakoshi

Tae kwon do is a way of life for constant self-improvement through the perfection of mind, body, spirit, and soul. Central to the attributes of a martial artist, whether physical or mental, is the achievement of do, the very principle of self-improvement.
—Sang Kyu Shim

Let's begin our discussion of American karate and tae kwon do with a general history of the martial arts. This isn't an easy task because the beginnings of the martial arts are clouded in dubious historical records as well as in legends and downright myths.

China

The most common legends tell of a Buddhist monk named Bodhidharma who is said to have traveled to China from his native India about 525. There, at the Shaolin Monastery, he found the monks in need of exercise and physical discipline. The legend describes how he began to teach them a system of exercise that came from his own ear-

From an early drawing of Bodhidharma, the reputed father of the martial arts.

lier training in yoga and Indian fighting methods. These exercises evolved into Shaolin Temple Boxing, also called *chaun-fa*—fist-way—or more commonly, kung fu. Incidentally, kung fu literally means "skillful activity" and can refer to areas other than just martial arts. During the centuries following the time of Bodhidharma, traveling monks and merchants introduced Shaolin exercises into other countries, including Okinawa, Japan, and Korea, where they evolved into other systems.

Although some scholars doubt that Bodhidharma even existed, there is still ample historical evidence to suggest that most martial arts indeed came from Chinese roots.[1] Because this is not a book on kung fu, I am not going to say much more about the Chinese systems here, but there are plenty of good books on the topic. One of my favorites is *Chinese Boxing* by Robert W. Smith.

Okinawa

Okinawa is the largest of the Ryukyu Islands, a string of islands off the coast of Japan. Karate was born here. It is said that in ancient times a style known simply as *te* (literally "hand") emerged from the influence of the aforementioned Shaolin Temple Boxing.

In 1609 the islands were forcibly annexed by Japan. During these oppressive times, *te* developed primarily in the three towns of Shuri, Naha, and Tomari. From these towns come the earliest recorded practice of Shuri-te, Naha-te, and Tomari-te, the forerunners of modern karate.

Although the Okinawans had been denied the use of bladed weapons by their own leaders, the developers of *te* managed to adapt farm implements into weapons. The five classical weapons of their practice were the *bo* (six-foot staff), *sai* (short forked truncheon), *kama* (sickle), *tonfa* (a wooden handle-like instrument), and *nunchaku* (wooden flail). Many Okinawan karate students learn these weapons in their practice, and there is even a separate martial art of weapons known as kobudo (old warrior ways).

By the 1880s the term kara-te was being used (the same *kanji* characters are sometimes also pronounced as "tode"). The translation was "China hand," acknowledging the Chinese roots of the art. In the early twentieth century, however, the spelling was changed to mean "empty hand" (a change most attribute to Gichin Funakoshi) as a way to make karate more acceptable to the Japanese public.[2]

Funakoshi was a public school teacher in Okinawa as well as a well-known karate instructor. In 1921 the Prince of Japan visited Okinawa and witnessed a karate demonstration by Funakoshi. The prince was so impressed that he invited Funakoshi to demonstrate in Japan. Originally Funakoshi had planned to return to Okinawa but soon decided to stay and spread karate in Japan itself.

Although Funakoshi was not the most senior karate practitioner in Okinawa, he was probably the best suited to popularize the art in Japan. He was educated and articulate. He also was familiar with Japanese customs and fluent in the Japanese language, while the other Okinawan masters were not. Funakoshi also was uniquely interested in promoting karate as a means of self-discipline and character development. This made his approach popular with the Japanese. In fact, it was not long before karate had gained a greater following in Japan than in Okinawa itself.

Karate has continued to evolve separately in both Okinawa and Japan. There is little formal communication between the many martial arts organizations in the two areas. This is due not only to generations of hard feelings but also to a difference in philosophy regarding sport karate. The Okinawans do not like tournaments, insisting instead on a tradition of kata (formal exercises) and self-defense practice. Today the major Okinawan schools are Goju-ryu, Shorin-ryu, Isshin-ryu, Shorei-ryu, and Uechi-ryu.

Japan

Although fighting systems collectively known as ju-jutsu (flexible way, sometimes spelled "jujitsu") have existed in Japan for hundreds of years, the modern styles of Japanese karate are derivatives of the Okinawan styles. In fact most reference books do not even list karate as an intrinsically Japanese art.[3] Many modern Japanese karate stylists differ with that view, however, and claim that their systems descend from the ju-jutsu schools and that their philosophies are continuations of the samurai code of Bushido.[4] We'll talk a bit about Bushido in chapter two. But Funakoshi and other Okinawans who traveled to Japan to teach, such as Choki Motobu and Chojun Miyagi, were not teaching the battlefield arts of the samurai but the civilian self-defense approach of Okinawan karate.

In the 1920s Gichin Funakoshi became friends with Japanese educator Jigoro Kano and was invited to teach at Kano's Kodokan (the headquarters for his newly founded system of judo). This added to karate's rapid exposure to the Japanese martial arts community. Funakoshi not only taught many judo students but also copied their colored-belt ranking system (the very first karate black belt was awarded in 1924).

It is said that Funakoshi did not intend to start his own system. He often said that he taught "just karate." But his style would become known as Shotokan, so called because of his pen name, Shoto (Pine Waves). Funakoshi said he gained inspiration from the pine trees waving in the winds off Mt. Torao near his hometown of Shuri, Okinawa. Torao, by the way, means "tiger's tail," so the tiger is the symbol of the

Shotokan style. Virtually all of the important masters of early Japanese karate studied Funakoshi's Shotokan either directly with Funakoshi or with his senior students.

While the general Japanese public was reluctant to associate with anything not Japanese in origin, they were eager to endorse anything popular with the upper classes. Soon karate became widespread on college campuses and with the "intelligentsia."

In 1936 karate teachers all over Japan solicited funds to build the world's first karate dojo. As a tribute to the 68-year-old Funakoshi, a plaque was hung over the door inscribed "The Hall of Shoto" (Shotokan). World War II brought a dramatic halt to karate practice in Japan. Many karate teachers were killed in the war, and the Shotokan hall itself was destroyed in a bombing raid.

Although today's karate practitioners don't like to talk about it, many of the early

A kobudo practitioner uses the *sai*.

Japanese teachers fought against Allied soldiers during the war. After Japan's defeat, General Douglas MacArthur banned martial arts practice in Japan, but many continued to train in secret. The ban was lifted in 1948, and some new schools began to open. In 1949 the Japan Karate Association (JKA) was founded to try to unify the schools, but by that time many had started their own systems and did not want to be under another instructor's control.

By 1951 the JKA had recognized the innovation of *kumite* (sparring), and the move toward making karate into a sport was under way in Japan. Interestingly, Funakoshi (Okinawan stylist that he was) disap-

Gichin Funakoshi, founder of modern karate.

proved of free-sparring, and Shotokan competitions weren't sanctioned until after his death at age 89 in 1957.

Today, karate is one of the most fragmented martial arts because of the many differences between styles and schools in Japan, Okinawa, and many other countries. Although there are many styles of Japanese karate (with more being introduced all the time), the four acknowledged major systems of Japan proper are Shotokan, Wado-ryu, Shito-ryu, and Japanese Goju-ryu. Kyokushinkai is another popular system, which became well known through the exploits of the late Mas Oyama.

Korea

Shaolin Temple Boxing made its way into Korea in the fourth century. At first the art was taught only on Korean temple grounds as a means to combine the physical and the spiritual. But by the seventh century, an art known as Subak was being taught to the general public as a means of exercise and self-protection. These were violent times because of conflicts between the three kingdoms in the land.

The kingdom of Silla emerged victorious, and in 688 most of the Korean peninsula was united under a central ruler. This period lasted 247 years and is considered a golden age in Korea's history.

During this time, a group that was critically important to the growth of the fighting arts in Korea was born. The Hwa-Rang warriors were an army of noble-born youths dedicated to the development of moral and patriotic ways. Their Hwa-Rang-Do code was in some ways similar to that of the Japanese samurai and was an essential element of

Silla's struggle to unify the country. References in Korea's oldest texts indicate that the Hwa-Rang warriors practiced Subak.

In 935 Silla was overthrown by the warlord Kyonghum, who established the kingdom of Koryo (from which the name Korea comes). Koryo was strongly militaristic in spirit, and all forms of martial arts flourished. The most notable systems were Subak and Tae Kyon.

After five hundred years, the Koryo Dynasty declined. The Yi Dynasty, which followed, held learning and scholarship in highest esteem. Confucianism replaced Buddhism as the political religion, and the military arts fell into disrepute. The arts of Tae Kyon and Subak barely survived by being passed on secretly from father to son.

The final blow came in 1909, when the Japanese Empire overran Korea and forbade the practice of not only the martial arts but also most Korean traditions. Many Koreans found conditions at home so oppressive that they traveled to other countries, some even to Japan itself, and for the first time were exposed to other forms of martial arts.

The end of World War II brought an end to the Japanese occupation. It also brought back to the country an intense feeling of national pride. As part of the national movement to restore Korean traditions, the martial arts were revived, and many teachers established their own schools. Most of them were eclectic stylists because of their exposure to techniques from many different styles during their exiles.

Some of the new systems' names were Kong Soo Do, Soo Bahk Gi, and Tang Soo Do. Each dojang (gymnasium) had different methods of training. Eight major kwans (schools) emerged between 1945 and 1953. Won Kook Lee opened the first post-war dojang, calling it the Chung Do Kwan (school of the blue wave). According to Jhoon Rhee, the "Father of American Tae Kwon Do," the Chung Do Kwan taught Tang Soo Do (way of the China hand).[5]

The conflict between the Communist forces in the north and the non-Communists in the south erupted into civil war in 1950. The cost to the

Way of the empty hand.

An ancient statue from Korea depicts a warrior in a martial arts-like stance.

Korean martial arts was high. Several of the leading teachers were killed, and others turned against each other. In 1952, in the middle of the war, a demonstration of the martial arts before President Syngman Rhee so impressed the leader that he ordered all South Korean troops to be trained in the martial arts.

Attempts had been made for years to unify the various kwans under a single name, but differences prevented it. Finally, in April of 1955, tae kwon do (the way of kicking and punching), a name suggested by Army general Choi Hong Hi, was approved. The name gained acceptance because of its similarity to the ancient name of Tae Kyon and because it indicated both hand and foot techniques.

There is debate about how many kwans joined the unification movement. In fact, some joined only to later drop out. Most of the schools didn't join until 1961, when the new military government decreed that the Korean Tae Kwon Do Association (KTA) be formed. General Choi was named the first president of the KTA.

In an effort to popularize the system, General Choi visited North Korea to demonstrate the art. Animosity still ran high between the Communists and non-Communists, and there were calls for Choi's resignation. In 1966 Choi left Korea and formed the International Tae Kwon Do Federation (ITF).

This split in the tae kwon do community forced instructors to take sides with one faction or the other. In 1973 the opponents of General Choi formed the World Tae Kwon Do Federation (WTF), which claimed to be the new "official" governing body of the art. With Choi's passing in 2002, the ITF and WTF have engaged in some limited unification talks, but because so many other tae kwon do organizations have been started in the past years (including at least three that claim to be the rightful heir to General Choi), it is doubtful that tae kwon do will ever be truly unified.

The Original Kwans (Founder, Year Founded)

Chung Do Kwan (Won Kook Lee, 1945)

Moo Duk Kwan (Hwang Kee, 1945)

Yun Moo Kwan (Sup Chun Sang, 1945)

Chang Moo Kwan (In Yoon Byung, 1946)

Chi Do Kwan (Yon Kue Pyang, 1946)

Song Moo Kwan (Byung Chik Ro, 1953)

Oh Do Kwan (Nam Tae Hi and Choi Hong Hi, 1953)

Ji Do Kwan (Gae Byang Yun, 1953)

The late General Choi claimed to be the one who suggested the name tae kwon do.

Who's on First?

If you can't figure out who's who in tae kwon do, welcome to the world of martial arts in the twenty-first century. Karate (both the Okinawan and Japanese versions) has never been united under a single banner. And did you know there are literally hundreds of systems of Japanese ju-jutsu (one of the oldest martial arts in Japan)? Additionally there are several systems of Brazilian ju-jutsu. Even aikido, once a single style, now has several different schools.

In China there were hundreds of "family" and "village" styles as kung fu developed over the centuries. (Although the Chinese government has standardized the name wushu for martial arts on the mainland, the term kung fu is still used in many other countries to refer to the myriad of Chinese systems).

Tae kwon do in Korea has undergone a startling transformation in the last fifty years. When the name was first coined in 1955, the Korean martial arts were very similar to the Japanese styles of karate studied by the Korean exiles in Japan before World War II.

In fact, the first forms that the kwans practiced were versions of Japanese and Okinawan kata (see chapter five). Not only did Koreans use the term "karate" to promote their arts in the United States and other countries, most kwans used an approximately equal mix of foot and hand techniques, just as in most styles of karate.

But soon the Koreans' feelings of patriotism (and their disdain for the Japanese because of the occupation of their country) led them to want to distance their styles from Japanese karate. Because the ancient art of Tae Kyon had been a kicking-oriented system, tae kwon do practitioners in Korea began to emphasize kicking. Also, there was an attempt to get tae kwon do (like judo before it) into the Olympic games, something karate had been attempting for years but could not achieve because of its fragmentation and infighting.

Martial arts practiced in the West come primarily from four Asian countries (although there are also Philippine, Vietnamese, and other martial arts): China (wushu, kung fu, and tai chi), Okinawa (karate, tuite, and kobudo), Japan (judo, aikido, ju-jutsu, and kendo), and Korea (Tang Soo Do, tae kwon do, and hapkido).

In order to convince the Olympic committee that tae kwon do was a completely different sport than karate, the governing masters changed the rules of competition, making high kicks the preferred techniques. Other Korean masters contend that the goal of Olympic recognition became too great a focus and that the art itself became diluted. However, when the Olympic Games were held in Korea in 1988 and tae kwon do

Kukkiwon "Olympic-style" tae kwon do, popular in Korea and much of the rest of the world, does not allow punches to the head or kicks to the groin. As a result, the vast majority of techniques are head-high kicks as opposed to the more equal mix of hands and feet that was common only a few years ago. Photo courtesy of Mark Williams.

Judo became an Olympic sport back in 1960. Perhaps it is the rules of competition that have made judo training one of the most uniformly consistent martial arts in its techniques and practice around the globe. Photo courtesy of Paul Tarrant.

was introduced as a "demonstration" sport, even the critics seemed proud to say they were tae kwon do practitioners. Tae kwon do became a permanent event in the 2000 Olympic Games. Karate and wushu continue to try to become Olympic sports as well.

Many instructors feel the overemphasis on sport and competition have taken the "do" (the philosophical principles) out of both modern tae kwon do and karate. As a result, many American teachers have formed their own new styles—much like the Japanese in the 1920s and 1930s and the Koreans in the 1940s and 1950s.

This is, admittedly, confusing to observers not familiar with the constant struggles within the various martial arts communities. These struggles have served to keep not just karate and tae kwon do but all martial arts constantly evolving and improving.

PROFILE: ED PARKER

Born in Hawaii, Ed Parker was the first American to found a legitimate system of American karate. He began training in kenpo in the 1940s under Frank Chow and later William Chow, under whom he earned his black belt. Parker served in the Coast Guard in Hawaii and went to Brigham Young University in Utah. He opened his first dojo in Pasadena, California, in 1956 and developed his own system of karate, calling it American Kenpo.

Being close to Hollywood afforded Parker the opportunity to teach several stunt men and actors, including Darren McGavin, Nick Adams, Audie Murphy, and, most notably, Elvis Presley. This association with celebrities gave Parker a platform to spread the martial arts in television and films, and he became an early ambassador for karate. Movie producer Blake Edwards added martial arts scenes to the *Pink Panther* films. Parker also founded his International Karate Championships, which served as the stage for many well-known martial artists such as Bruce Lee, Mike Stone, Chuck Norris, Allen Steen, and Joe Lewis. Ed Parker passed away in 1990.

See www.americankenpo.com. Photo courtesy of Ed Parker Jr.

Karate and Tae Kwon Do in America

Most martial arts historians put the date of the first karate instruction in America as 1946, when Robert Trias, a World War II veteran who had studied karate overseas, began teaching private martial arts lessons in Phoenix, Arizona. Two years later Trias formed the United States Karate Association, the first organization of Asian martial arts in the United States.

A collection of early American karate pioneers. Back row: Allen R. Steen, George Mattson, Ed Parker, Hidetaka Nishiyama, Robert Trias. Front Row: J. Pat Burleson, Bruce Lee, Anthony Mirakin, Jhoon Rhee.

The first national exposure to karate, however, occurred in 1952, when karate instructor Mas Oyama toured the country fighting professional wrestlers and boxers. His demonstrations of kata were met with skepticism by American audiences, but his feats of board and brick breaking caused great interest. Oyama was a large, muscular man, and his power demonstrations inadvertently popularized karate as a kind of superhuman and mystical art.

Another American karate pioneer, Ed Parker, studied kenpo under William Chow in his native Hawaii. In 1956 he opened the first karate school in California. Later Parker would form his own version of karate, calling it American Kenpo.

In 1959 Peter Urban opened the first karate school in the New York area (in Union City, New Jersey). He also created his own style, American Goju, and created quite a controversy by proclaiming himself a tenth degree black belt.

A few years earlier, in 1956, a young third degree black belt named Jhoon Rhee arrived in Texas to introduce America to the Korean martial arts. At the time, Rhee taught Tang Soo Do (most Koreans had not yet accepted the name "tae kwon do"). His first class was at the Air Force base in San Marcos, close to San Antonio. Tang Soo Do didn't mean anything to Westerners, so Rhee used the term "karate" because it was much more recognizable to Americans who had heard tales of "karate experts" from servicemen returning from Japan and Okinawa. Rhee soon started teaching at the University of Texas, and his first black belt out of that class would turn out to be one of the biggest pioneers of the martial arts in the United States—Allen R. Steen, who became known as the "Father of Texas Blood 'n' Guts Karate" because of his chain of schools and his reputation as a champion and trainer of champions.

Steen opened the first karate school in Texas in Dallas in 1962. In a few years Steen had established a chain of schools across Texas, while Rhee had moved on to Washington, D.C., to build his own chain. By then Rhee had switched to the term "tae kwon do" to promote his art, but Steen and his followers in the Southwest continued to call their style "karate."

An early photo of Jhoon Rhee demonstrating power.

This pattern was repeated all across the United States in the late 1950s and early 1960s. S. Henry Cho, an East Coast tae kwon do pioneer who arrived in 1961, says that Americans already knew of karate, so he just called his style by that name. Cho actually taught a system called Kong Soo Do (literally "empty hand") at the time. He also wrote the entry for "karate" in the World Book Encyclopedia. Students of Rhee, Cho, and other Koreans like Richard Chun and Jack Hwang became instructors themselves in a few years, and "Korean karate" became firmly established.

Dennis Goetcher scores on Jim Butin in an early tournament. Notice that the fighters wore no gloves.

Of course, Japanese instructors also were coming to America to find fame and fortune. Shotokan stylist Hidetaka Nishiyama came in 1961, as did Teruyuki Okazaki. Richard Kim, a Korean who was an expert in Okinawan karate, also came to the United States in the early 1960s and taught many American martial arts pioneers. American-born black belts were only interested in promoting karate as an effective fighting method and had no interest in political maneuverings back in Asia.

California's Chuck Norris (left) and Texan Skipper Mullins were two of the early heroes of American karate in the 1960s.

In fact, many American-born martial arts practitioners started their own organizations to promote the martial arts in America, but promoting the martial arts in this country in the 1960s was a tough sell. Although karate and judo were regularly seen on television and in the movies, they were usually clouded in mysticism. Not only did Americans not understand the martial arts, they didn't think they were effective. Thus the early practitioners faced constant challenges from street fighters, even in their own schools.

That's one reason the early tournaments were so brutal. Americans seemed obsessed with proving karate was a superior method of fighting. They were quick to adapt any technique that "worked," whether it was from the Japanese or the Koreans (or even a Chinese system, if they could find it). These Americans had no loyalties at all to the "Japanese" or "Korean" way of doing things. For example, the Koreans would never publicly admit to adapting techniques from Japanese styles, but Americans were quick to do so if the techniques seemed effective.

Steen tells the story of getting knocked out by a ridgehand in a particularly fierce match. Out cold for almost five minutes, when he woke up he asked what technique had hit him. He couldn't believe it was a ridgehand because he had been taught that was a weak "Japanese" technique. He taught it from then on. Perhaps this was one of the reasons many Americans parted ways with their Asian instructors during the late 1960s and 1970s. In fact, when the Korean government changed the tae kwon do training forms in the mid-1970s, practically none of the American tae kwon do practitioners made the switch. Most of them didn't follow the turmoil going on in the Korean tae kwon do world—they were too busy establishing the American style.

The American style was unique indeed. In 1965 Jhoon Rhee persuaded ABC's *Wide World of Sports* to cover his National Karate Championships in Washington, D.C. However, the heavy contact and bloodshed of the title bout between Mike Stone and Walt Worthy shocked the producers, who aired only a few moments.

Although the rules in the 1960s did not allow for "contact," they were generally disregarded. The techniques may have been crude by today's standards, but the fighters were arguably tougher. It was not uncommon for a competitor to receive a broken nose or ribs and be expected to come back and dish out the same to his opponent.

Some of the greatest champions from this rough and tumble era include Allen Steen, Mike Stone (who reportedly went undefeated in every black belt match he ever fought), J. Pat Burleson (who won the very

Bruce Lee was famous for both his movie roles and his controversial methods.

first national championship), Skipper Mullins (named one of the top-five fighters of all time by his peers), Joe Lewis (the first full-contact champion), and Chuck Norris (a top-five fighter who went on to have a successful movie and television career).

Because few Asians entered competitions in the United States, many Americans viewed the Japanese and Koreans with skepticism. "Why," they wondered, "were they afraid to actually compete with American-born and trained karate practitioners?" Adding to the rift between Asians and Americans was the cultural difference. Many Asian teachers were irritated by American students' habit of questioning their instructions: "Why do we stand this way?" "How does this block work?" They were used to students who would practice whatever they were told without question. It was common in Japan to repeat the same

Bill Wallace and Roy Kurban were two of the American karate champions of the 1970s and 1980s.

technique for months or even years before being allowed to learn another one. Americans wanted to learn as quickly as possible. According to tradition, "explanation" was not part of the teaching method of the martial arts, which only served to disenchant most American students.

This ultimately led to what karate historian Jerry Beasley calls the "contemporary era" of American karate, which began in the early 1970s. It could, perhaps, be epitomized by the teachings of Bruce Lee, ironically a Chinese-born martial artist coming out of a traditional background (wing chun). Lee may have become famous for his movies, but he made an even greater impact in the martial arts community with his characterization of the old methods as "the blind following of tradition." He suggested that while training forms or kata might be good for learning and practicing certain principles and techniques, they were not very useful in self-defense or fighting. Whether Lee was correct (and I do not necessarily agree with him), his call for more realistic training methods incorporating Western boxing and wrestling into his Chinese martial arts base became very popular. He called his approach Jeet Kune Do (way of the intercepting fist) and often pointed out that this was not a "style," as he didn't like the concept of "only one way" of doing things, advocating instead a "whatever works" approach.

In 1973 Jhoon Rhee introduced foam rubber sparring pads, which allowed for semi-contact without the risk of injury that had accompanied bare-knuckled fighting. In fact, the very first time I ever wore padded gloves was during my third degree black belt examination in 1973. More competitors started entering tournaments in the mid- to late

1970s, as sparring was now safer (and because there were more students). American martial arts magazines featured stories on tournaments and on the champions of the day. Bill Wallace, nicknamed "Superfoot" because of his incredibly fast kicks, became the leading karate fighter.

Athletic competition had long been an accepted practice in the West, and the tournament scene became the primary method for promoting karate in the United States. The American style came to be closely associated with a sporting approach. Ultimately, however, the sport image stalled, and

A 1970 photo shows the Texas Competition Team of Candy Simpson, Demetrius "Golden Greek" Havanas, Skipper Mullins, and Keith Yates.

karate tournaments were not established as an alternative to football, boxing, or even golf. To this day, the only people in the stands at an American karate tournament are the families of the participants.

Even though tournaments are held all over the country today, there are very few truly national events. Judges are often ill prepared, and controversies about outcomes are not infrequent. Even most of the martial arts magazines have stepped back from sport-oriented coverage. Many of the sport karate heroes themselves have found that there is more to be gained, both personally and commercially, from turning back to an emphasis on the character-building aspects of martial arts.

J. Pat Burleson, the first American karate champion and a feared, no-nonsense competitor, says that American karate came full circle in the 1990s. According to Burleson, instructors who teach only the sporting aspects are doomed to repeat the failures of the past. He says that while the heavy-contact era of 1960s competition was necessary to

Raymond McCallum (right) was one of the champions of the 1970s who hailed from Texas.

establish karate in the United States, the only thing that will keep the martial arts growing is an emphasis on traditional philosophy and discipline.

It is difficult to predict how karate will grow and develop in this country in the twenty-first century. The martial arts community is a widely diverse collection of systems, and with the proliferation of commercial dojos (schools), there is a greater and greater emphasis on the moneymaking side of the arts.

With the passing of some of the great pioneers of American karate like Robert Trias and Ed Parker, their once-dominating organizations have splintered into several factions. Contrary to what some groups claim, there is simply no single organization that can truthfully claim to represent a majority of American karate or tae kwon do practitioners.

It may be that the martial arts attract people with strong personalities, who seldom yield their viewpoints to others when it comes to unification; however, American karate, which was once ridiculed for being non-traditional, has established itself as a tradition unto itself and has emerged as one of the most influential and powerful martial arts systems in the world.

Profile: ALLEN R. STEEN

Allen Steen is known as the "Father of Texas Blood 'n' Guts Karate." In 1959 he started training with Jhoon Rhee while a student at the University of Texas. By 1962 he was a black belt, opening the first commercial dojo in the Lone Star State in Dallas. He won many national titles in his fighting career (including the 1966 Internationals, when he defeated Chuck Norris and Joe Lewis in a single evening).

Steen's real fame came as an instructor and business leader. Most of the champions of the 1960s and 1970s were trained by Steen, including Demetrius Havanas, Fred Wren, and Skipper Mullins. His chain of schools spanned the state of Texas and beyond. Many of the innovations in marketing the martial arts came from the business acumen of Allen Steen. He retired early from the martial arts and went on to establish a successful career in the oil-well business and become recognized as a champion skeet shooter.

See www.allensteen.com.

Nam Seo Kwan Tae Kwon Do

Compared to today, when many instructors claim to have trained hundreds of black belts, Allen Steen had relatively few—probably no more than fifty who trained personally under him all the way to black belt (although he can legitimately claim to have partially trained dozens more, and his family tree certainly extends into the thousands, with so many of his students training other black belts). But the fact remains that he was a hard taskmaster, and not many could pass to black belt under his intense qualifications.

Keith Yates as a nineteen-year-old second degree black belt in 1970.

I feel fortunate to have trained under Steen and his "blood 'n' guts" system of karate. By the mid-1970s, however, he had sold his schools and moved into other endeavors. Many of his students continued teaching classes, in settings ranging from small YMCA groups to large commercial studios. In 1976 I formed the Southwest Tae Kwon Do Association (STA) to provide sanction for some of these independent clubs. I certainly didn't feel like I was the only Steen black belt qualified to start such an organization, but I did have the respect of the other instructors, and the association grew over the years. In 1996, the twentieth anniversary of the STA, I realized that with members in several states, we had outgrown our name, and I rechristened the organization the American Karate and Tae Kwon Do Organization (A-KaTo).

Our version of tae kwon do teaches basically the same system that Allen Steen learned from Jhoon Rhee, although many elements have been added and improved on by both Steen and myself over the years. For example, I began training in the early 1980s with ju-jutsu instructor and author Ted Gambordella. I had never concentrated much on grappling or ground techniques, and it was fascinating to learn and practice ju-jutsu wrist locks and takedowns. I've incorporated many of those techniques into our curriculum.

Steen had required a "specialty" for advanced degrees of black belt—something that the individual had specifically learned for that rank. I chose weapons for my second and third degree exams. However, there were no instructors teaching traditional weapons in those days in north Texas, so I had to learn on my own. As soon as I was able to begin training with some actual kobudo (weapons) teachers, I incorporated those techniques into our advanced training.

Keith Yates (left) spars with the late, great Demetrius Havanas during one of the black belt fighting classes in Allen Steen's old East Dallas school.

Like many traditional stylists, I have been concerned that many instructors have shifted from a martial "art" emphasis to a martial "sport" one. While acknowledging that tournaments are a valid training aspect, I have always taught the traditional aspects of the martial arts and sought to make sure that our foundation remains self-defense and individual self-improvement.

With the recognition afforded tae kwon do by the Olympics, the general public has been understandably confused when faced with the difference between "traditional" tae kwon do and the newer "sport" tae kwon do. The training patterns have changed over the years, the sparring rules are different, the entire approach has shifted dramatically. The term tae kwon do simply doesn't reflect the art as we teach it. That is why I've made a point of referring to my approach as "American tae kwon do."

But, alas, "American tae kwon do" and "American karate" have become overused terms these days. It seems like everyone in an open tournament claims to practice this generic brand of "American" martial arts. Many are very talented martial artists, but others are not. To some, the term "American tae kwon do" is an indication of a "watered-down" approach to the martial arts. I don't totally agree with that evaluation, but I understand it. That is why, several years ago, I came up with a "style" name to go with my approach—one that distinguishes

Allen Steen collapses the heavy bag with a flying side kick as a class of police officers watch.

it from the other American-style schools. Nam Seo Kwan (naam-sah-kwan) literally means "School of the Southwest," and was named after the original title of the association. Not all schools within A-KaTo teach under the name Nam Seo Kwan, but I do require the schools to maintain an eclectic but traditional approach to tae kwon do or karate, keeping the emphasis on the "art" of the martial arts and definitely with a bottom-line emphasis on self-defense.[6]

In no way do I claim that our system of tae kwon do is superior to any other approach. I have always said that it is the individual rather than the style that makes a skilled martial artist; however, it is my hope that within the framework of our system many talented and dedicated martial artists will continue to emerge and develop.

A Martial Arts Style Chronology

This timeline is offered only to allow you to put some of the history of modern martial arts into perspective. There are thousands of schools of martial arts all over the world, so we can only list a few of the more well-known styles.

1882—JUDO, Jigoro Kano

The first "modern" martial art. Kano, a ju-jutsu master, substituted the word "do" (which conveys a meaning of a "path" or "way of life") for the word "jutsu" (which means "warrior art").

Keith Yates has had the opportunity to work with many great martial artists over the years. Left: Chi Surichuti, Yates, Dan Inosanto. Center: Richard Shoffit, Eric Lee, Yates. Right: John Corcoran, Yates, Joe Lewis.

1924—SHOTOKAN, Gichin Funakoshi

The first modern karate style. Funakoshi introduced the Okinawan art of karate into Japan. In order for it to be more accepted by the Japanese, he changed the concept of "kara," which was first written with a ideogram meaning "Chinese," into one that meant "empty" but was still pronounced "kara."

1930—SHITO-RYU, Kenwa Mabuni

A major Japanese karate school.

1939—WADO-RYU, Hironori Ohtsuka

Another major Japanese karate school.

1941—KENPO, James Mitose

The first karate style created outside of Asia—in this case, in Hawaii.

1942—AIKIDO, Morihei Ueshiba

Like Jigoro Kano, Ueshiba changed the name of a "jutsu" art, aiki-jutsu, into a "do" art.

1947—KAJUKENBO, Adriano Emperdo

Another style created in Hawaii; the name is a combination of the terms "karate," "judo," "kenpo," and "boxing."

Karate pioneer Jim Harrison founded his Bushidokan system in the 1960s.

1954—ISSHIN-RYU, Tatsuo Shimabuku

A major Okinawan karate school.

1955—TAE KWON DO, Choi Hong Hi

Not really created by General Choi, but named by him. He was the first president of the first tae kwon do association in Korea.

1956—AMERICAN KENPO, Ed Parker

The first style created by an American in the United States.

1961—KYOKUSHIN KAI, Mas Oyama

A notable style because it is a Japanese system founded by a Korean.

1961—HAPKIDO, Yong Shul Choi

Now taught in many tae kwon do schools as the "self-defense" part of the curriculum.

1966—KUK SOOL WON, In Hyuk Su

Actually founded in the United States by this Korean-born immigrant.

1966—AMERICAN GOJU, Peter Urban

Created by Urban after breaking away from the Japanese Gojo-ryu school.

1967—JEET KUNE DO, Bruce Lee

Lee never claimed it was a style of martial arts, but merely a way of practicing the arts.

1969—WON HOP KUEN DO, Al Decascos

Created by a champion of many early American karate tournaments.

1972—KUKKI TAE KWON DO, Several masters, including Dr. Kim Un Yong

When the Kukkiwon was built in South Korea, the World Tae Kwon Do Federation moved its headquarters there. This is the system most noted for being the "Olympic" sport.

1973—JHOON RHEE TAE KWON DO, Jhoon Rhee

The system created by the man who introduced Korean martial arts into the United States.

1973—CHUN KUK DO, Chuck Norris

The system taught by Norris's United Fighting Arts Federation.

1976—AMERICAN TAE KWON DO NAM SEO KWAN, Keith D. Yates

Means "School of the Southwest."

1980—SONG AM TAE KWON DO, Haeng Ung Lee

The official style of the late Master Lee's American TKD Association.

Profile: CHUCK NORRIS

Most people think of Chuck Norris as a movie and television star (and the subject of all those Chuck Norris "tough guy" jokes), but he was one of the biggest names in martial arts competition before his first acting gig. He was a six-time undefeated World Professional Middleweight Karate Champion. He was *Black Belt* magazine's "Fighter of the Year" in 1968, "Instructor of the Year" in 1975, and "Man of the Year" in 1977.

Norris has starred in twenty-four movies and in the long-running television series *Walker, Texas Ranger*. He is the founder of the United Fighting Arts Federation with more than two thousand black belts around the world. He is also the founder of the KickStart Foundation, which takes the martial arts into public schools and teaches "at-risk" kids the benefits and character-building aspects of the martial arts. An author with several books and a regular online presence, Norris continues to teach and speak around the world.

See www.chucknorris.com.

Milestones in American Karate and Tae Kwon Do

1850s to 1900s—Kung fu is practiced in Hawaii and some parts of California, but it is not taught to non-Chinese. (Hawaii did not become a U.S. state until 1959.)

1946—Robert Trias opens first karate school in Phoenix.

1952—Mas Oyama tours America breaking boards and bricks.

1954—Ed Parker begins teaching kenpo in Utah.

1956—Ed Parker opens a school in California.

— Atlee Chittim sponsors Jhoon Rhee's arrival in Texas to introduce the Korean arts in the United States.

1957—Frank Goody, Jr., begins teaching in Colorado.

— Don Nagle returns from Okinawa to teach in Jacksonville, Mississippi.

1958—George Mattson starts the first Uechi-ryu karate classes in America in Boston.

— Elvis Presley starts taking karate in Germany while stationed there with the U.S. Army. He will go on to earn his black belt and promote the martial arts in film and concerts.

1959—Peter Urban opens his first Goju-ryu school in New Jersey.

1960—S. Henry Cho opens the first tae kwon do school on the East Coast, in New York City.

— Jack Hwang begins teaching tae kwon do in Oklahoma City.

— Steve Armstrong begins teaching Isshin-ryu in his garage in Seattle.

1961—Shotokan instructors Hidetaka Nishiyama and Teruyuki Okazaki arrive in the United States.

— Nishiyama forms the All American Karate Federation.

— Richard Kim begins teaching Shorinji-ryu in San Francisco.

— *Black Belt* magazine first published.

— John Pachivas begins teaching Shuri-ryu in Miami Beach, Florida.

1962—Jhoon Rhee moves to Washington, D.C., to begin his chain of schools.

— Allen Steen opens the first karate school in Texas in Dallas.

— Richard Chun begins teaching tae kwon do in New York City.

— Chuck Sereff begins teaching tae kwon do in Colorado.

— Bob Yarnall opens a Shorin-ryu school in St. Louis.

1963—Mike Stone, while still a brown belt, begins his undefeated karate sport career.

— Jim and Al Tracy start the first karate franchise, "Tracy Brothers Karate."

1964—J. Pat Burleson wins the first recognized national karate championships in Washington, D.C.

1964—Ed Parker begins his International Karate Championships in California.

— Bruce Lee begins accepting non-Asians at his school in Oakland, California.

— First accredited college karate course in the United States is founded by T. Ohshima at the Institute of Technology in Pasadena, California.

— Jack Hwang opens his dojang in Oklahoma City.

1965—Dan Ivan sponsors Fumio Demura's arrival in Los Angeles to teach Shito-ryu.

— Roger Carpenter opens a karate school in Wichita, Kansas.

**Mike Stone vs. Pat Burleson.
Photo courtesy of Pat Burleson.**

Joe Lewis fights Bill Wallace. Photo courtesy of Joe Lewis.

1966—Joe Lewis wins first place in both kata and sparring at Jhoon Rhee's U.S. Nationals in Washington, D.C. He will go on to win this tournament three more times.

— Allen R. Steen wins the International Karate Championships in California by beating both Joe Lewis and Chuck Norris.

— Bruce Lee co-stars in the television show *Green Hornet*, playing Kato.

1967–68—Chuck Norris wins the Internationals two years in a row, establishing himself as one of the greatest karate fighters of the 1960s.

1968—Aaron Banks holds his first World Professional Karate Championships in New York City, paying $600 to each of the four winners (Joe Lewis, Mike Stone, Chuck Norris, and Skipper Mullins).

1970—Pat Johnson creates the penalty point system for excessive contact, heralding the end of the "blood 'n' guts" era of American karate.

— Joe Corley and Chris McLoughlin hold the first "Battle of Atlanta."

1971—Bruce Lee co-stars in the television show *Longstreet* as the blind detective's martial arts instructor.

1972—Bill Wallace rises to the top of the sport karate world to become the number one–rated fighter.

— Jhoon Rhee introduces foam sparring pads.

— The first "martial arts" television show, *Kung Fu*, airs.

— Karate is introduced as a fully accredited physical education course at Southern Methodist University in Dallas by Keith Yates.

— The movie *Billy Jack* features Hapkido teacher Bong Soo Han as star Tom Laughlin's stunt double.

1973—First semi-contact karate tournament, sponsored by Mike Anderson, occurs in St. Louis and is the first to require Jhoon Rhee's padded gloves and boots. Howard Jackson wins the grand championship.

— Shortly before the U.S. release of *Enter the Dragon*, Bruce Lee dies.

1974—The Bruce Lee and Chuck Norris fight scene in the movie *Return of the Dragon* sparks Americans' interest in the martial arts.

— The Professional Karate Association is formed to sanction full-contact fights.

— First full-contact karate championships occur in Los Angeles. This sport will become kickboxing. Winners include Joe Lewis and Jeff Smith.

— Tae kwon do recognized as an amateur sport by Amateur Athletic Union.

— The G.I. Joe action figure gets the "kung fu grip."

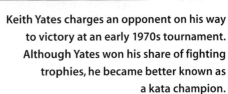

Keith Yates charges an opponent on his way to victory at an early 1970s tournament. Although Yates won his share of fighting trophies, he became better known as a kata champion.

1976—Keith Yates forms the Southwest Tae Kwon Do Association.

— Chuck Norris appears in his first starring role in *Breaker, Breaker*.

1977—Benny Urquidez wins his fortieth straight professional karate bout, becoming an international celebrity (he even has a Japanese comic book series).

— Howard Jackson becomes the first karate champion to launch a successful boxing career (he finishes 14-1-2).

1982—Jhoon Rhee's nephew, John Chung, wins *Black Belt* magazine's Forms Competitor of the Year award by practicing his uncle's musical forms.

1984—*The Karate Kid* creates a great influx of children into karate schools.

1988—Tae kwon do first appears as a demonstration sport in the Seoul Olympics. American Arlene Limas wins a gold medal.

— Jean Claude Van Damme stars in *Bloodsport.*

1990—The *Teenage Mutant Ninja Turtles* movie keeps interest in the martial arts going among kids.

1991—Point karate and kickboxing champion Kathy Long is named *Black Belt* magazine's Woman of the Year and is inducted into the Hall of Fame of *Inside Kung-Fu* magazine.

1992—Tae kwon do fails to become a regular event in the Olympics but appears as a demonstration sport again in Barcelona.

1996—The Southwest Tae Kwon Do Association becomes the American Karate and Tae Kwon Do Organization.

2000—Tae kwon do finally becomes a permanent event in the Olympics.

—"Extreme" martial arts, combining karate with gymnastics, become a popular demonstration sport in mainline tournaments.

2001—Jackie Chan's *Rush Hour 2* ends its U.S. domestic run with a take of over $226 million, making it the highest-grossing martial arts movie ever.

Obviously there are many people and events not presented in this brief listing. This is meant only to give the reader a brief overview of some of the milestones of karate and tae kwon do in the United States.

Questions from Chapter One

■ Who was the Indian Buddhist monk who is said to have established martial arts–type exercises at the Shaolin Monastery in China? Approximately what year was that?

■ The common name for many Chinese arts is kung fu. But what was the ancient name that literally means "fist way"?

■ What was the ancient art of Okinawa that evolved into karate?

■ What are the five classic weapons of kobudo?

■ Who is credited with changing the name "kara-te" (China hand) to "kara-te" (empty hand)?

■ The same man originated the first "modern" karate style. What is its name?

■ Name three styles of Okinawan karate.

■ What is the ancient martial art of Japan that is translated "flexible way"?

■ The Kodokan is the headquarters for what martial art that was founded by Jigoro Kano?

■ Name three styles of Japanese karate.

Keith Yates works with Dallas Cowboy offensive lineman, Brian Baldinger, at a 1981 NFL mini-camp.

■ What was the name of the ancient army of young Korean warriors dedicated to patriotism?

■ The name Korea comes from what ancient kingdom?

■ When did Japan invade Korea?

■ When the United States liberated Korea, many martial arts halls soon opened. What is the Korean term for a gymnasium or training hall?

■ The Chung Do Kwan taught a system known as the "way of the China hand." What was that system's name?

■ What year did tae kwon do get its name?

■ Who suggested it?

■ Most martial arts in the West come from which four nations?

■ Who is said to be the first American to teach martial arts in America (in 1946)?

■ Who toured the United States in 1952 breaking boards and bricks?

- Who introduced the Korean martial arts to the United States?
- Who was the "father" of Texas karate?
- Name three champions of the early years of American karate competitions.
- Name a couple of martial artists who made the leap to the silver screen.
- Because the modern Korean approach has taken a turn toward the sporting aspect, what do many instructors in the United States call their own approach?

TWO

Philosophy

It takes a year to harvest a crop, ten years to see the full beauty of a tree, and fifty years to make a man.

—Korean proverb

The Precepts of Karate-Do

1. In karate, start with a bow and finish with a bow.
2. There is no first attack in karate.
3. Karate is a great assistance to justice.
4. Know yourself first and then others.
5. Spirit first, techniques second.
6. Be ready to release your mind.
7. Accidents come out of idleness.
8. Do not think that you can learn karate only in the dojo.
9. It will take your entire life to learn karate.
10. Karate-ize everything.
11. Karate is just like hot water. If you do not give heat constantly, it will again become cold water.
12. Do not think you have to win. Think, rather, that you do not have to lose.

Gichin Funakoshi, the "Father of Modern Karate"

13. Victory depends on your ability to tell vulnerable points from invulnerable ones.
14. Move according to your opponent.
15. Consider your opponent's hands and legs as you would sharp swords.
16. As soon as you leave home for work, think that millions of opponents are waiting for you.
17. Low stance for beginners, natural stance for advanced students.
18. Practicing a kata is one thing, and engaging in a real fight is another.
19. Do not forget: (1) light and heavy application of power, (2) expansion and contraction of the body, (3) slowness and speed of techniques.
20. Devise at all times.

One of the reasons people begin martial arts training is the promise of more than just fighting techniques. They have heard that martial arts teach character-building aspects such as self-discipline, self-confidence, and respect for others. No one would argue that these are not needed in American society today, but are the martial arts a proper way to develop character? Can fighting techniques, of all things, really teach philosophy?

The answer is seen in hundreds of years and millions of practitioners. Yes, karate, tae kwon do, and the other martial arts can indeed impart to their participants a sense of discipline, honor, and respect. At least, they can if they are taught properly.

Karate, traditionally taught, is the development of the whole person. The *mind* and the *character* of the individual are just as important as the *body*. I am sure you've heard of "mind, body, spirit."

It has been said that there are three types of people in the world: those who make things happen, those who watch things happen, and those who wonder what just happened. The key to becoming a leader who makes things happen is self-confidence combined with the right abilities. Karate certainly teaches self-confidence. In addition, the self-discipline and focused learning attitude developed in the martial arts lead to the development of abilities not only in the karate school but also in everyday life. This carryover into everyday life is what makes the martial arts so attractive as a vehicle for developing character.

The Martial Arts Should Make You a Leader

The Unconsciously Unconscious
   Those who don't know what's happening.
The Consciously Unconscious
   Those who watch things happen.
The Unconsciously Conscious
   Those who make things happen.

According to an old Chinese proverb: "It is said martial artists need strength and speed. But if one man defeats many men, how can it be a question of strength? And if an old man defeats a young man, how can it be a question of speed?" I do believe that success in the martial arts involves strength and speed, but as this proverb indicates there is something more—whether you call it emotional intensity, a desire to win, or self-confidence, it can supersede even the advantages of youth and size.

Some martial arts instructors refer to the ancient code of Bushido when they teach these concepts. Bushido was the Japanese samurai way of life, which included a code of behavior that some compare to the "chivalry" of the European knight. There were many aspects to the code of Bushido, such as discipline and loyalty, but perhaps the best known is the total acceptance of the possibility of death (this comes from Zen Buddhism). Each moment was to be experienced as if it were the last moment before death.

Many Americans, grasping for a bit of culture and philosophy for their martial arts practice, have adopted the samurai "outlook" for their modern karate practice. They name their schools "Samurai Martial Arts Club" and speak about adhering to the code of Bushido.

Bushido stressed death and duty. The samurai's purpose in life was defined by honing his mind and body through austere training. But to an actual samurai, Bushido also was about the exclusivity of the samurai class; the samurai saw himself as far above the common man. Only samurai could carry swords, and they could kill peasants without facing any consequences.

In light of these historical facts, I think it would be better for the modern martial artist to emulate not Bushido but the more modern concept of budo.[1] Literally, budo means the "way of fighting," but a better translation might actually be the "way of avoiding fighting." As Japan entered the modern age, there was less need for actual combat and a greater desire for harmony. The old warrior arts (known as bujutsu) became more concerned with character development, transforming bu-jutsu to bu-do.[2] Arts like ju-jutsu and aikijutsu gave way to judo and aikido (see chapter one).

In Korean-based arts, this same emphasis is brought into the modern arena through the teaching of the principles of the Hwa-Rang warriors. The modern "tenets of tae kwon do" reflect this attitude, as do the precepts of karate as set forth by Funakoshi.

One of the most important concepts of modern budo is that of respect for others. It is this principle more than any other that keeps the trained martial artist from using his skill in anything other than a legitimate self-defense situation.

The competent instructor teaches students that they are responsible for their own actions. Martial arts ultimately result not only in the refinement of technique but also in the advancement of mental control. People who are in control are less likely to use their techniques to harm others. They are responsible both in the figurative and in the literal sense.

This is what makes traditional karate and tae kwon do more than mere sports. Other sports may teach physical and mental discipline, but they don't necessarily teach respect and self-control—in fact sometimes just the opposite. Baseball players who take illegal drugs to enhance their performance and then justify it before investigators place all of modern society on the stand. Why do we place so much emphasis on winning? Is being the best in any sport worth sacrificing our morals, our character, our very selves to that end?

Martial arts instructors everywhere proclaim the character-building aspects of the arts, yet many of them turn around and practically force their students into tournament competition and then wrongly encourage them to "go all out" to win. This defeats the very purpose of martial arts—to strive to do your best but accept whatever comes with strength and discipline of character.

Does it show strength of character to complain to the judges that they didn't see your backfist? Does it reflect positively on your character when you proclaim—loudly—that the officials cheated you and that you could really beat that so-and-so in a "real" fight?

American society is fixated on the winner. I remember when the Buffalo Bills went to the Super Bowl four straight times. No other team has accomplished that feat. They were one of the best teams in the history of professional football. Yet because they didn't win the Super Bowl, many considered them failures.

An athlete trains all his or her life for a chance at the Olympics or for the "pros." One fall on the ice or one failed pass or kick can break a career. She can go from being a contender for the Gold Medal to fifth or sixth place. He can go from being the guy who could win the Super Bowl to the guy who lost the Super Bowl. Perhaps these pressures are to be expected in professional athletics, but they should not be forced upon the average martial arts student—especially young ones. Day-to-day effort is worth more in the dojo and in life than one super moment. Especially when that one moment may never come!

Some martial arts students may feel that if they can't be the best of the best, then they will quit training altogether. Bruce Lee said, "In every passionate pursuit, the pursuit counts more than the object pursued." In other words, the training is more important than the trophy.

As martial artists, indeed as human beings, we should aim for excellence but not for perfection. We should want to be *our* best, not *the* best. As Funakoshi would say, the essence of karate isn't about victory over an opponent but triumph over yourself. You have to conquer yourself constantly in your training. You may not always want to go to class—you're too tired or too busy—but you must have the will to practice, to train, to better yourself.

The Olympic Gold Medal, the Super Bowl Ring, the first place sparring trophy—all are worth striving for but none is worth sacrificing everything else we have and are. The pursuit of excellence is the reward in and of itself.

The experiences a martial arts student has in his or her training can be of tremendous value in meeting the requirements of everyday life. There is a state in the martial arts called, in Japanese, mushin or "no mind." That is the place of unconscious consciousness.[3] Once your mind no longer has to concentrate on individual movements and techniques, it is free to prepare for the challenges of combat or of life. This level of focus usually occurs at the brown or black belt. You don't have to think of what to do anymore—you just do it!

When you can perform your techniques in this state of "no mind" (simply without thinking about them), you realize that your mind is capable of applying physical actions with almost no mental effort, giving you supreme confidence that you can be in control in all circumstances.

I like to say that "self-knowledge" results in self-confidence. You have to have an understanding of your own strengths and weaknesses. As the great martial arts philosopher Harold "Dirty Harry" Callahan said, "A man's got to know his limitations." Karate and tae kwon do practice should lead to a greater understanding of not only your strengths (e.g., I am disciplined, I am young and flexible) but also your weaknesses (e.g., I have short legs, I have a hard time remembering details). So I tell my students to work on maximizing their strengths, certainly, but also to work on minimizing their weaknesses.

Martial arts are a total pursuit, meaning that you must learn to control not only your physical body but also your intellect and emotions. If so applied, your training can calm you in the face of a charging opponent in a *gi* or in a dark alley, as well as in the face of stress at school or work. Self-confidence enables you to find everyday life a little less daunting. Life is, after all, a struggle, and only in having the confidence to face the struggles can we grow and mature.

Over and over I have seen karate and tae kwon do training serve to mature my young students (and a few older ones as well). Setting goals for yourself and helping others achieve their own goals teaches you the "long" view of life.

The Tenets of Tae Kwon Do

Tae kwon do emphasizes courtesy, humility, integrity, perseverance, self-control, and indomitable spirit (Figure 2-2). These characteristics, which are often taught in tae kwon do schools, typify the philosophy of all martial arts. (Some older lists don't include the trait of "humility," but I like to include it because I think it's a good characteristic to teach and because it makes a neat acrostic, C-H-I-P-S-I.)

여의
염치
인내
극기
백절불굴

Tae Kwon Do tenets

The Lessons of Humility

There are many tales of samurai warriors for the Japanese stylist to recite, but there aren't many legends from the Korean historical perspective. The following is one of the few that I heard several years ago.

During the Koryo Dynasty (which the modern name "Korea" comes from), there was a master of Tae Kyon (the ancient martial art of the land) named Lee Pyung. In fact, he was so skilled that he had been appointed the leader of the royal guards who protected the king.

One day, when Lee Pyung was visiting a temple, he came across one of the Zen masters from his childhood. Wanting to impress the old man, Lee Pyung began to boast of his accomplishments and his position. "I am well-known as the greatest Tae Kyon practitioner in the country," he proclaimed. "There is no one I have not or could not beat."

The master only smiled and replied, "There are at least two whom you have not defeated."

Taken aback, the younger man said, "Please master, I do not wish to be disrespectful, but I have trained and practiced much since you knew me. I could easily defeat all who would challenge me."

"Then I myself challenge you," the old master responded, and Lee Pyung found himself in a battle right there in the temple.

Although the Tae Kyon practitioner was full of confidence and skill, every time he tried a jumping or flying kick, the Zen master would sidestep or duck completely out of the way. Lee Pyung would frequently find the monk's robes swirling in front of his face, blinding him as he attacked. His efforts grew more frantic and desperate. Finally he admitted his defeat and bowed before the master.

"You are obviously one whom I cannot defeat," he acknowledged. "But who could possibly be the other person you spoke of who can conquer me?"

"You are strong but not all-powerful," replied the monk. "One who conquers many warriors is strong, but one who conquers himself is all-powerful. While you may defeat others, you cannot defeat your own ego."

Then Lee Pyung understood that he would have to defeat his own pride before he could rightly be called the greatest of the Tae Kyon masters.

Do not let your ego and pride in your accomplishments prevent you from recognizing one of the deeper lessons of learning how to fight—humility and the realization that there is always someone better than you.

The martial arts have been proven to enhance self-esteem and self-discipline. In fact, organizations like Chuck Norris's KickStart Foundation actually teach these concepts interwoven into martial arts classes to "at-risk" youth in public school settings with dramatic results.

To win one hundred battles is not the highest skill. To subdue the enemy without fighting is the highest skill.

—Gichin Funakoshi

Perfection lies not in the destination but in the journey.

—Bruce Lee

The real enemy or obstacle isn't something out there. The real enemy is this person right here, inside yourself. If you can learn to control that person, no one or nothing else matters.

—Haeng Ung Lee

A wise man accomplishes his goals without a love of glory.

—Kwai Chang Caine (in the television show *Kung Fu*)

Figure 2-4

Meaning of the A-KaTo Logo

Our American Karate and Tae Kwon Do Organization logo consists of the yin-yang (um-yang in Korean) symbol set in a triangle (Figure 2-4).

The yin-yang symbol is an ancient representation of opposites. In the martial arts, it refers to the interflow of hard and soft, kicks and punches, empty hand and weapons techniques.

The triangle's three sides reflect the three aspects of martial arts training: the intellectual, the physical, and the emotional (or mind, body, spirit). These three aspects also are reflected in our student pledge: "Knowledge in the mind, honesty in the heart, and strength in the body."

Patience

This story is a paraphrase of an old martial arts tale.

A young man went to an old master and asked, "Sensei, how long would it take to be a master like you if I trained eight hours a day, every day?"

The white-haired one replied, "Oh, perhaps twenty-five years."

"But I cannot wait that long," said the boy. "What if I trained every waking hour and only slept five hours a night?"

"If you are willing to practice that hard, then fifty years," replied the sensei.

"You don't understand," said the lad. "I said I would train even longer and harder."

"No, it is you who has no understanding," said the master. "You see, impatience is a stumbling block to learning. If you want to truly master something like the martial arts, you can only do so with a patient attitude."

Honor

American military veteran Forrest Morgan, in his book *Living the Martial Way*, notes that honor is a central tenet of what he calls "warriorship." He says honor is common to all warrior groups regardless of culture. Honor involves virtues like loyalty, self-control, justice, and courage.

To expand on just a couple of these, Morgan argues that because martial artists have the physical skills to hurt other people, restraint or self-control is a crucial component of a warrior's honor code. That is the difference between a martial artist and a common thug.

Certainly, your karate and tae kwon do training develop a sense of courage. You have to be able to face larger and perhaps more skilled opponents on the mat and in a tournament ring. But Morgan defines the courage of a warrior as more than just facing a potentially dangerous situation. He says it is having the courage, the willpower, to do what is right in a given situation.

Self-worth

Not long ago, some thieves broke into a department store in a major city. Actually, they weren't thieves, because they didn't steal anything.

They just switched the price tags on hundreds of items throughout the store. Confusion reigned the next day. The real irony, however, was that the deed wasn't detected for almost two hours. Some people got incredible bargains: a $500 suit for $89 or a diamond ring for $50. On the other hand, some people got ripped off big time: $200 for a $59 dress, $300 for a $99 camera.

What does that say about people's ability to recognize value? Many of us must rely on price tags to tell us the worth of an item. How does that relate to the price tags we put on other people?

Here's another story from the news pages. During the major league baseball strike of 1994, Seattle Mariners reliever Dave Graybill, a re-placement player and a Glendale, Arizona, firefighter, helped rescue eighteen-month-old twin babies from a burning house. Later that same day, he worked two scoreless innings in a 6-5 Mariners win over the Chicago Cubs. The question I'd like to ask is: "For which of those two acts could he get paid a six-figure income?" Why are baseball players worth big bucks while firefighters who save little babies worth only a fraction of that kind of money?

Do you sometimes judge a person's worth by externals? If a man is dressed shabbily, do you categorize him a certain way? If a woman is thin, beautiful, and well dressed, do you consider her more valuable than a woman appearing just the opposite?

Of course we all say, "I wouldn't do such a thing," but let's face it, we do it more often than we would like to admit. That's one thing I love about the martial arts. Everyone looks the same in a uniform. The doctor and the ditch digger are indistinguishable. Our opinions about fellow students are based on their actions and attitudes in class rather than on their wardrobe or social status.

But I'm speaking here about more than just our opinion of people; I'm suggesting you ask yourself how you value others: Do you put an imaginary "price tag" on someone because she is shy? How about the mentally handicapped? Homely people? Instructors, do you spend more time with the athletically gifted students?

One of the main principles of karate or tae kwon do is respect for others. This is developed through the respect students must show their teachers and fellow students. Hopefully, over a period of time, this attitude of respect through the bowing, the "yes sirs," and the displays of humility will work its way into a student's psyche. Soon the martial artist really does find herself beginning to show respect to others out of force of habit.

Influence

Controversial basketball star Dennis Rodman once told an interviewer that he didn't want to be a role model. He said he wanted to be free to "be himself" without having to worry about influencing anyone else.

Well, regardless of what Rodman wants, he is, by nature of his position, a role model. In truth, we all have a certain amount of influence on others. Some people only affect a few—friends, siblings, co-workers. Other people, including martial arts instructors, have influence on dozens, hundreds, or even millions.

Alfred Nobel was a successful entrepreneur who invented, among other things, dynamite. One day his brother died, but a newspaper mistakenly thought it was Alfred instead. He awoke the next day to read his own obituary in the morning paper. It said he was the inventor of dynamite and other weapons of destruction. It even called him a "merchant of death."

Nobel was shocked and saddened to find out that in spite of all the positive things he had done in his lifetime, he would be remembered for such negatives. He determined to dedicate his life to peace, and thus was born the Nobel Peace Prize.

Most of us wouldn't have a second chance to change the perception that others have of us and to rewrite our own obituary. At your funeral, people won't stand around and talk about the kind of car you drove, but they will remember your character, your love for others, and how you made them feel.

Because of our contact with others, martial artists are visible influencers. This is especially true if you are an upper belt or a teacher. You simply can't escape that fact any more than Dennis Rodman can say he isn't a role model.

If you can admit you are indeed an influencer of others, how can you do the best job of it? I like to think of a role model's influence as being divided into three essentials: an ethical aspect, which I call "courage"; an emotional element or "heart"; and an intellectual aspect or "brain." These three elements might remind you of something else— the lion, the tin man, and the scarecrow.

The author of *The Wonderful Wizard of Oz*, L. Frank Baum, says in the preface to his famous book that he was trying to create a more positive influence on children than the fairy tales by the Grimm brothers popular in the day. If you have ever actually read any of the Grimms' tales, they are surprisingly scary stories meant to frighten kids into proper behavior (children who don't obey their parents are torn limb from limb, for example).

To return to our premise of the three-pronged appeal of a proper role model, first there is the ethical appeal. Why do I call that "courage"? Well, it often takes courage to stand up for what you know is right. It takes bravery to keep your word when there are temptations to do otherwise. Your ability to keep your promises and to maintain your convictions establishes your credibility. Role models must be credible.

Secondly, we have the emotional appeal of the influencer. That is seen in your "heart"—your ability to care for others. Your credibility will answer the question when others ask, "Can I trust you?" But they also will want to know, "Do you care about me?" The answer to that will determine what kind of role model you will become.

The third prong is the intellectual appeal. Simply put, the more you know, the more you can teach others. The question asked by those you would try to influence is: "Do you know what you are talking about?" You cannot lead someone to a place where you have never been.

The tough times we experience in our training as martial artists are but a microcosm of real life. You get knocked down, but you keep coming back. You flunk a test, but you take it again. We have a responsibility to the lower ranks to show them tenacity not only in our training but also in how we approach life. We should have the courage of our convictions, a heart for other people, and a brain full of knowledge to face unforeseen challenges. With these three elements in the proper balance, we can influence those around us and be positive role models.

Martial Arts and Religion

I think it is interesting that the Apostle Paul uses the warrior as a metaphor in discussing how self-sacrifice and discipline are required to develop spiritual characteristics, thus winning heavenly crowns (I Corinthians 9:25–27). He is saying that he trains with the intensity of a martial artist, if you will, not to win a contest but to conquer himself.

It's true that most people don't think of Christian spiritual growth when they picture a karate practitioner. Indeed many in the martial arts use the Asian concept and phrase "mind, body, spirit." That suggests a deeper spiritual or religious component to practice, and many Americans start getting nervous at that point.

"Will my child be indoctrinated into Buddhism?" "Are we going to be meditating to connect with otherworldly spirits?" These are fair questions. After all, the martial arts are historically linked to Asian philosophies and religions. But the real question should be, "Does karate, tae kwon do, judo, kung fu, or any martial art have to be taught in such a context?"

So many people have asked me these questions that I decided to do my seminary master's thesis on the subject of "The Spiritual Aspects of the Martial Arts." After lots of research, my conclusion is that martial arts—at least the way they are taught in practically every dojo on Main Street, USA—do not indoctrinate students into the tenets of Asian religions.

In fact, I would dare to say that most karate and tae kwon do instructors couldn't even carry on a coherent discussion about Zen or Taoism, let alone teach any of their principles or philosophies. However, that doesn't mean you shouldn't be aware of what those approaches teach. So here, in a woefully inadequate nutshell, are the basic ideas.

Zen

In this offshoot of the more popular Mahayana Buddhism, Zen followers seek to attain "enlightenment" through meditation and austerity. In fact, Zen is sometimes called Meditative Buddhism. The founder of Zen is said to be the Indian monk Bodhidharma (remember him from chapter one?) who came to China around the year 600.

Because Zen developed in ancient China, it contains many elements of Chinese philosophy. And probably because of these diverse elements, Zen is really hard to define—even the experts don't exactly agree on how to best describe it.

Zazen is the practice of seated meditation and is a fundamental part of the religion. It is often combined with koans, questions such as, "What is the sound of one hand clapping?" Koans are not meant to be directly answered—they are paradoxes used to get adherents to stop thinking logically. Through this meditation and introspection, practitioners turn inward to find their own enlightenment and, hopefully, achieve the state of nirvana (also called satori).

Taoism

To a Taoist, the "Tao" is all of nature, and the main attitude toward nature should be one of noninterference. Maybe they were the original environmentalists! The philosopher Lao Tzu is said to have claimed, "Do nothing and there is nothing that will not be done." In other words, by being passive you can harness the power of nature.

Tao literally means "path" or "way." Adherents of Taoism try to "go with the flow" of life. Think of Yoda saying, "Use the force!" At first Taoists taught that there is no afterlife or supreme being, and no need to worship deities. But by the second century, the Chinese had built the philosophy into a religious set of rules and even sacrifices.

The "three jewels of the Tao" are compassion, moderation, and humility. Like Zen, it is hard for a Western mind to understand exactly what it's all about. The yin-yang symbol is associated with Taoism because it indicates the balance in the universe. The little dots of opposite color represent the idea that there is a bit of the opposing force within the major element, i.e., there is a bit of female within the male, male within the female, good within the bad, bad within the good, and so on.

Internal vs. External

One thing to be aware of is that karate and tae kwon do are considered "external" styles, i.e., "just kick and punch the bad guy," and thus less likely to delve into Asian philosophies than the so-called internal styles like aikido and tai chi. It seems that the softer the techniques (that is, evading, sweeping, and throwing the bad guy), the more emphasis on what some call "harmonizing" with his ki energy (next page).

This whole concept of universal energy is widespread in Asian religions. So if you'd rather not have to deal with these kinds of emphases, stick to an external style. Even at that, talk to your instructor about his or her own take on "the force."

My bottom line is—if you are a Christian or just someone who isn't interested in Eastern religions, you probably don't have anything to be concerned with in your typical American dojo. I wouldn't even be afraid of the term "spiritual" if the emphasis is on controlling your emotions and building solid character rather than "connecting with God." That said, I personally like to use the phrase "mind, heart, body" just to be clear to my students where I am coming from.

Ki

Ki

Ki is the Japanese (and the Korean) translation of what the Chinese refer to as Chi (sometimes Qi). It is an energy that flows through and sustains the universe—think again of "the force" in *Star Wars*. It's a nebulous concept, sometimes translated as "breath," "energy," or "spirit." You see this philosophy in acupuncture (needles stuck into your skin to cause your Chi energy to reflow) and in the martial art of aikido (harmonizing with an opponent's energy to misdirect or throw him to the ground). It comes from the pantheistic idea that there is no personal God but rather an impersonal force that governs the world we live in.

Hard vs. Soft

The many martial arts styles also can be divided into physically hard versus physically soft schools. This is similar to the internal/external division, but the emphasis is on "physically" hard or soft. Some styles, like karate and tae kwon do, tend to strike an opponent with kicks and punches. This is a hard style of fighting. The softer approaches may, using leverage, push an attacker off to the side and allow her to either lose her balance or fall to the ground. Westerners may find this hard/soft separation an easier concept to grasp than internal/external.

Hard and soft labels aren't just for demarcation of physical techniques. You can take a hard-core approach to your training, working out seven days a week and twice on Saturdays. Or you might take a softer approach, going to the dojo just once or twice a week. It all depends on what you want to achieve. On one hand, if your goal is to be a national champion, or if you have a black belt exam coming up, you might want to make that Herculean effort. If, on the other hand, your desire is to stay in shape and perhaps relieve a little stress, then you can enjoy the journey as much as the destination.

Profile: JHOON RHEE

Grandmaster Jhoon Rhee is the man who introduced the Korean martial arts to America. But I'll bet you didn't know he is also known as the "Father of Tae Kwon Do in Russia," having traveled extensively in the former Soviet Union countries and established more than sixty-five schools in the region.

He is also the originator of the padded sparring gear that helped to popularize tournament competition and made the martial arts accessible to children in the early 1970s. And Rhee, a talented musician, was the first to put martial arts forms together with musical scores, creating what he called the "martial ballet."

His longtime classes in Washington, D.C., have afforded him the opportunity to teach and mentor hundreds of politicians (from both sides of the aisle). Presidents of corporations and of countries have honored him. George Bush Sr. named him one of his "Thousand Points of Light" for his contributions to society. In 2000, Rhee also was named one of the two hundred most influential American immigrants on a list that included Alexander Graham Bell and Albert Einstein.

Always an outstanding example of discipline and strength, he was known in his early years for his fantastic demonstrations with Bruce Lee featuring a trademark triple jump side kick. For years he has amazed crowds with his hundred push-ups in sixty seconds.

Today, Grandmaster Rhee travels the world with his message of "truth, beauty, and love" to promote world peace and understanding.

Martial arts without philosophy is merely street fighting.
—Jhoon Rhee

Jutsu vs. Do

Many modern practitioners of karate think of *jutsu* as the "combat" versions of the martial arts and *do* as the "sport" version, but that is an oversimplification of the facts. It is true that jutsu is the older approach and is concerned with combat applications, but because it emphasizes techniques for the ancient battlefield, many of its applications, if literally applied, are useless for a contemporary street fight (you will not fight armored soldiers, horsemen, or samurai sword–wielding opponents, for example).

And while do (pronounced "doh") is the more modern term and certainly is more associated with competition-oriented styles like judo and kendo, it has much more to do with a certain way of looking at life than with winning a tournament.

In another part of my life, I teach graphic design at a graduate school. There is a difference between knowing how to apply some of the principles of design, like "contrasting graphic elements" and "alignment," and actually having an eye for artistic beauty. There are mechanical techniques and principles that can be learned by any of my students interested in graphic design, but for them to really be "artists," they must have that unique spark of creativity and a desire to express the inner self in their work. This, in a way, is the difference between the technique (jutsu) and the art (do).

Jutsu / Do

A History of Do

In 1497 civil war broke out in ancient Japan, and part-time soldiers became hardened professionals who trained and killed for their "lords." Though popularly known as samurai, a more accurate term would be bushi or warriors. They practiced the bujutsu or warrior arts. Each group would concentrate on a certain approach (depending on the leanings and skills of the head teacher). These became the individual schools known as ryu. The beginnings of the ryu are cloaked in mysticism (due to the religious nature of the era) and in secrecy (no one wanted the enemy to know their strengths). Contrary to what some modern martial artists think, the classic weapons of the bushi were the sword, spear, halberd, and bow, not the empty-handed techniques of modern karate. The arts of the ryu included kenjutsu (art of the sword) and kyujutsu (the art of the bow).

As peace finally settled on Japan with the fall of the feudal system in 1868, the bushi realized they had to change with the times or their whole way of life would die. Narrow clan loyalties gave way to a much broader sense of national unity. The warrior arts (jutsu) widened in scope to encompass Japanese spiritual and moral tenets with a new goal of improvement of the individual and the betterment of society. In an attempt to transfer the virtues of the warrior mindset to the general public, the combative elements were toned down and sporting aspects were introduced.

Many masters of the ryu thus changed their focus and even changed their system's names, adding the suffix "do." For example, Jigoro Kano founded judo out of ju-jutsu, and Morihei Ushiba created aikido from aikijutsu. Both of these masters stressed the need to defend oneself without causing injury to an opponent (if possible). They also both wrote extensively on the character-building aspects of the martial arts.

From Gichin Funakoshi to Choi Hong Hi, and from Ed Parker to Jhoon Rhee, the great founders and masters of the modern do have stressed character over competition and "the way" over the winning.

The bottom line is, you teach the jutsu, but you model the do.[4]

Profile: SKIPPER MULLINS

A former U.S. Marine, firefighter, paramedic, and top-ten world champion, Lewis "Skipper" Mullins is one of the pioneers of martial arts competition in America. He began his training under Allen R. Steen in 1964 at a National Guard Armory in Dallas.

Mr. Mullins won scores of tournaments, including seven world titles, and is acknowledged as the best kicker of his era. Someone once said that Mullins could hit you with a front leg round kick from across the room before you even saw it coming. He was a part of the 1969–1972 undefeated U.S. professional karate team that traveled the world convincing other countries that Americans were the best in the fighting business. In 1967 he competed in a tournament in New York City on Friday night, a tournament in Dallas on Saturday, and one in Los Angeles on Sunday. He won two out of the three. In 1987 *Black Belt* magazine named him one the top five fighters of all time.

He taught Marines and FBI trainees at Quantico, Virginia, and his Texas students included national champions like Demetrius Havanas, Ronnie Cox, and Raymond McCallum (oh, and me, too).

See www.skippermullins.net.

Profile: JOE LEWIS

Joe Lewis is perhaps the best karate fighter America has ever produced. He earned his black belt in record time in Okinawa while stationed there as a U.S. Marine. In fact, he won the black belt division of the U.S. National Championships less than two years after taking his first karate class. His subsequent list of national and world titles wouldn't fit on one page.

Mr. Lewis has been called the "Father of American Kickboxing," winning the first world heavyweight championships and then fearlessly promoting the new sport around the globe. He was named *Black Belt* magazine's "Fighter of the Year" in 1975 and "Co-Instructor of the Year" in 1986. He was voted the best karate fighter of all time by his peers. He is in literally dozens of Halls of Fame and was the first recipient of the National Association of Professional Martial Artists Life Achievement Award.

Some people don't know that Mr. Lewis was an accomplished musician as a youth and had at one point considered a musical career, but the Marine Corps called and he never looked back.

Today a tenth dan black belt, he has developed an extensive teaching curriculum that has contributed to the careers of countless champion martial artists through his personal appearances and DVD series. He developed and integrated a comprehensive, definitive teaching method, which involves a confidence-building thinking process. Its usage helps the practitioner to create mental energies to produce greater conviction and overall effectiveness exercised during the execution of any martial arts skills.

See www.joelewisfightingsystems.com.

Photo courtesy of Mike Allen and Joe Lewis.

Questions from Chapter Two

- State a couple of Funakoshi's "precepts of karate-do."
- What was the samurai code of life?
- What are the "tenets of tae kwon do"?
- What is the ancient symbol of opposites?
- The modern Japanese martial arts can collectively be called the "ways of fighting" or _____.
- When you don't have to think of what to do anymore—you just do it—it's called the "state of no-_____."
- What is the Japanese translation for the Chinese term "Chi"?
- Which is the older term: "jutsu" or "do"?
- Which of those terms encompasses an emphasis on the character-building aspects of the martial arts?
- What is the Japanese term for "training hall"?

THREE

Procedures

To permit murder when one could have prevented it is morally wrong. To allow a rape when one could have hindered it is an evil. To watch an act of cruelty to children without trying to intervene is morally inexcusable. In brief, not resisting evil is an evil of omission, and an evil of omission can be just as evil as an evil of commission. Any man who refuses to protect his wife and children against a violent intruder fails them morally.

—Norm Geisler, theologian

There are unwritten customs to be obeyed in a martial arts class. Every student, regardless of rank or seniority, should be aware of and obey these rules. Of course, if they are unwritten, how do you learn them except by having them passed down from seniors to juniors? Well, I'm going to give you a shortcut and write some of them down for you in this chapter. Remember that traditions and manners not only set the mood but also help the beginning student learn and practice the primary martial arts principles of discipline and respect.

Bowing

Bowing, Uniforms, Belts, and Promotions

Bowing

Every class starts with bowing. The bow symbolizes respect for others as well as self-discipline. As Americans practice it, there is no religious significance to the bow. In fact, the Asian bow is often compared to the Western handshake. The martial arts bow does, however, involve more than just a "greeting." You should bow to your teacher to show the respect he deserves because of his own dedication to karate and to you as his student. For the same reason a subordinate in the military will initiate a salute to a superior out of respect.

There is an odd notion in modern schools that you should never take your eyes off your opponent, so you must bow with an awkward upward bend in your neck, allowing you to eyeball your adversary (I think this can be traced to an old Bruce Lee movie). But in Japan or Korea it is considered disrespectful to keep your head up when you bow. Certainly, however, keep a proper distance, which will afford you the opportunity to keep the other person within your peripheral vision.

And this curious habit of tournament competitors who slap their hips or, worse, their rear ends is the antithesis of humility! Just place your hands against your thighs and slowly bend forward, holding the bow for a second as a show of humility and respect.

Uniforms

Okinawan karate practitioners wore a fundoshi, which is basically a loincloth. Today's students, thankfully, wear a *gi* (Japanese) or a *tobak* (Korean). According to martial arts historian Dave Lowry, the spiritual

Traditional *gi*

Tobak

significance of the traditional white uniform (purity and/or emptiness) was attached to the white color of the *gi* (early *gi* were actually beige) after it was adopted for general use in the early twentieth century.[1] Some modern tae kwon do stylists have adopted a pullover top called a *tobak* for competition. Many American instructors allow uniforms of various colors.

Whatever you call them in your school, these loose-fitting, pajama-like outfits are well suited to vigorous physical activity. Besides, they help the students feel like real martial artists.

Take care of your uniform. Keep it washed and pressed, because a clean and orderly environment is critical for proper karate training.

And no one wants to train with a person whose uniform smells like a gym locker. How you keep up with your appearance is a reflection of how you feel about yourself.

Belts

It is said that in ancient times the kimono belt of the advanced karate practitioner would turn black with age and accumulation of dirt. Whether or not this is true (and it probably isn't), the black belt *has* become the accepted symbol of the stage at which a student becomes a teacher. Perhaps it is because of this myth that many martial artists never wash their belt.

Actually, wearing colored belts is a modern innovation that most attribute to Jigoro Kano, who founded judo in 1888.[2] Gichin Funakoshi instituted it into his karate system in the 1920s, and it has been a method of signifying skill level ever since. The wearing of colored belts to indicate rank has been a successful idea, especially for Westerners, as American students like to have some sort of visible recognition of their achievement.

Most belt colors are recent additions. For example, when I started back in the 1960s, we only went from white to green to brown and finally to black. Today there are myriad colors, and belts vary from school to school. In all schools, however, the student starts out with a white belt (a symbol of emptiness) and progresses through several stages until black belt. Belt rank is important in a modern karate or tae kwon do class. It is similar to military rank, with all the regulations and symbols of respect that you might suspect.

These are typical belt color divisions for what I'll call the seven major categories of rank in a karate or tae kwon do school. Not all schools have all these colored belts:

1. Beginning: White / Yellow / Orange / Gold
2. Intermediate: Purple / Green / Blue

3. Advanced: Brown / Red
4. Beginning Instructor: First and Second Black Belt
5. Advanced Instructor: Third and Fourth Black Belt
6. Master Instructor: Fifth, Sixth, and Seventh Black Belt
7. Grandmaster Instructor: Eighth, Ninth, and Tenth Black Belt

Receiving a new belt promotion

Black belt ranks are even more confusing. The Shotokan school's black belt degrees, for example, originally went up to only fifth dan (pronounced "don"). Judo's founder was awarded an eleventh dan (it was white to show a return to purity). The WTF does not have the tenth dan.

Promotions

Promotion to your next rank requires memorization of certain requirements, usually consisting of training patterns, kicks, self-defense demonstrations, sparring, and sometimes board breaking. Criteria for promotion include more than just physical techniques. Attendance and attitude are also critical, especially at the intermediate and advanced levels. Most schools have time requirements for each level, although in some systems students cannot test until the instructor says they may (which can be months or years).

The Class

When the student enters the workout area for the first time, he or she must bow in. Students will likewise bow when leaving the area.

At the command "one line" or "line up," the students line up according to rank—highest ranks to the right—in ready position. When there are children and adults of the same rank, the kids line up to the junior side (left) of the adults. On a signal from the senior black belt, the highest-ranking student will give the formal commands. On "charyo" ("attention" in Korean) or "kiotsuki" (Japanese), the students will bring the left foot to the right and bring their hands to their thighs. On "kyungye" ("salute" in Korean) or "rei" (Japanese), they will bow respectfully—maintaining the bow until the senior black belt rises.

If a student is late and misses a bow, she should stand at the entry to the school or at the edge of the mat and wait for the proper recognition and bow from the instructor. If a student needs to leave for any reason, he must gain permission. If the class is in progress and a more senior instructor enters the class, the highest-ranking black belt calls the students to attention to bow to him or her.

Any time a student wishes to ask a question, he should raise his hand and address the instructor by "Mr. Cox," "Mrs. Goodspeed," etc., before asking. After the answer, the student should respond to the black belt with a bow.

Before sparring, the students bow to the black belt and to each other before beginning. If a brown or red belt is conducting the sparring session, the students are to bow to each other but not to the brown or red belt.

Each school has its own protocols, so you should familiarize yourself with your own instructor's requirements.

The Dojo

The Japanese word "dojo" and the Korean word "dojang" both roughly mean a gymnasium or training hall.[3] Whatever you call your school, a clean and orderly environment is critical for proper training. Even

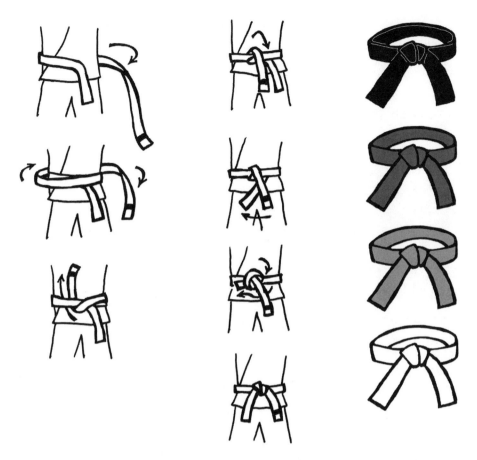

Wearing the uniform and belt: place one end of the belt against your abdomen. Wrap around your waist twice. Tuck the end of the belt under and up behind both layers. Fold the belt down, and tuck the left side under the right. Now make a loop up, around, and through. When finished, both ends of the belt should hang down the same length.

more important than the physical surroundings are the attitudes of the teacher and students. If you are looking for a school, it will be beneficial to speak with the instructors, the students, and the parents of students to find out more about the school.

If you encounter a braggadocious teacher who tells you all about his or her accomplishments instead of what you will be learning, that's a good sign that the instructor is not focused on the students.

Back when I was a "junior" green belt, in the dark ages of American martial arts, we had to dye just the ends of our belts instead of the entire belt as the adults did (note that belt around my waist). Yes, everyone had to dye his own belt, even using dye remover to get rid of the previous coloring.

Unfortunately there really are instructors like the "bad sensei" in many karate movies. You want to find a teacher who cares about the students, one that can communicate with them on a level they can understand (not all black belts can effectively teach children, for example).

Watch a class before you sign up. A good karate class reflects the philosophical attitudes we just discussed. Discipline must be obvious, but an extreme military-like atmosphere often stifles enjoyment, and after all, karate classes should be enjoyable, or you won't want to come back.

Remember that maturity in the martial arts, or in life for that matter, is not acquired overnight, and a good teacher will take time for his students. That means making time for students' questions. In some traditional classes, students are never allowed to speak, let alone ask questions. Most American instructors, however, will take the time to make sure everyone understands why they are doing a technique and how they should do it.

A good dojo will stress the three primary aspects of karate training: *kihon* (fundamentals), *kata* (repetition of technique), and *kumite* (two-man exercises or sparring).

A good teacher will not indulge the impatient student who is "bored" by the "same old thing" but will help her students overcome the boredom by refining the moves they already know. This comes through kihon and kata. A traditional dojo will stress the basics.

Sixty years ago I knew everything. Now I know nothing. Education is the progressive discovery of our own ignorance.

—Will Durant, historian and Pulitzer Prize winner

Grasshopper, seek first to know your own journey's beginning and end, but in this seeking, know also patience.

—Master Poe (in the television show *Kung Fu*)

Profile: JIM HARRISON

When Bruce Lee said Jim Harrison was one of the "most dangerous men in America," he was talking about his fighting abilities, and no one I know would dispute that sentiment. Mr. Harrison was a three-time U.S. Karate Champion, three-time All American Champion, and an undefeated light-heavyweight kickboxing champion. He was also the coach of the 1974–1976 undefeated U.S. Professional Karate Team.

He was a police officer in St. Louis serving on the "Special Violence Squad" that conducted operations in the most dangerous parts of the city. No doubt many of his renowned self-defense seminars are based on the lessons learned in the streets. Mr. Harrison has earned black belts in judo, ju-jutsu, aikido, and in several styles of karate. He is the founder of his own Bushidokan system.

An avid outdoorsman, he took second place in the Northwest Paraskiing Championships, competing in the twenty-to-twenty-five-year-old division when he was in his fifties. A little-known fact is that he stunt doubled for Robert Culp in the television series *I Spy*.

See www.bushidokan.net.

The black belt

The Black Belt

Funakoshi awarded the first Japanese karate black belt in 1924. Many Okinawan and Korean martial artists wouldn't adopt the practice until decades later, and some Chinese arts still do not have a belt system.

Many myths have grown up around the "black belt." One popular misconception, for example, is that there is a single karate "organization" that regulates black belt promotions. Alas, that is not the case, and a black belt doesn't mean the same thing in every karate or tae kwon do school.

For example, if you go to an American tournament, you are sure to encounter a black belt under the age of ten or a fourth or fifth dan under the age of twenty. I don't want to create more controversy than there already is about little kid black belts, but what does it say about the sophistication of your style if a child who can barely tie his own shoes can make a black belt in it? How hard are you willing to work for something that is attainable by a second grader? Allen Steen wouldn't promote anyone to black belt under the age of seventeen (I was one of his youngest). I have made concessions to modern times and the many kids we have in classes today, and so I have established my minimum age for black belt as twelve (although the vast majority of mine have been older than that).

We have other requirements for black belts in the A-KaTo. Allen Steen believed that the testing for first degree black belt should be the most physically demanding examination of one's martial arts career. I agree. Therefore, our first degree black belt examination consists of a demonstration of *all* the lower belt requirements as well as the forms and other techniques for the black belt itself. It can take several hours to perform everything (although I have already given much of the exam ahead of the actual test date by evaluating a candidate's teaching skills, attitudes toward others, and character).

Extensive free-sparring is a part of the physical examination, including multiple opponent sparring with up to four persons at once. We also expect a thorough knowledge of kata and their meaning as applied to self-defense, and we expect the candidate to have worked out with several different instructors to encourage the student to have a broad exposure to the martial arts. We also include a written test covering the history and philosophy of the martial arts.

Because at black belt level the student has reached instructor status, we require that candidates have several months of teaching experience as an assistant instructor under the supervision of a senior black belt. Black belts can additionally earn an "instructor certification."

Beginning karate students are naturally quite rank conscious and are often surprised to hear a first or second dan refer to herself as a beginner. But first degree or shodan (Japanese) and chodan (Korean) really means "first step."[4] In Japanese, for example, a stairway is called a *kaidan*, or series of steps. That lowest rung of black belt is really just a beginning step into the more sophisticated levels of the martial arts. The kyu/dan (junior/senior) ranking system comes from the ancient Chinese game of *go*. In Japanese martial arts, kyu (pronounced "cue") level practitioners are students below the rank of black belt. Kyu ranks count down from ten to one while dan ranks count up from one to ten.

Beyond the First Step

A-KaTo higher black belt testing assumes that the candidate has begun to delve into more sophisticated techniques, including weapons and grappling as well as more advanced forms. So while these exams may not be as physically tough, they are more demanding in that they require a higher level of skill and preparation. Go to our website (www.akato.org) to see more about our requirements.

Remember that not all organizations have the same set of regulations about higher black belt levels. In general, however, most associations consider ranks above fourth dan "positional" and are awarded on the basis of "time in grade" and contribution to the martial arts community. These levels are purposefully rare and indicate extreme dedication to the martial arts.

At advanced ranks, black belts are expected not only to have mastered their own primary art but to have extensive experience in other martial arts as well. In fact, in the A-KaTo, an earned black belt ranking in another style is required for a sixth dan.

"Master" Rankings and Titles

Different systems have various requirements for high ranks and titles, causing much confusion in the martial arts world. Many instructors in both America and Asia (although there are more controls over the practice in Asia) have been guilty of bestowing grand-sounding titles on themselves.

There is a story about George Washington that I like. In refusing the title of "king," he said, "I would rather be spat upon than called 'Your Majesty.'" He preferred to be called "Mr. President."

Personally, I just have my students call me "Mr. Yates," but because many instructors like titles, here's some information on their proper use. Japanese karate has a long list of titles for high-ranking instructors. Not all black belts receive them. Incidentally, these titles are used only on certificates. The holders are still addressed as sensei or "teacher" in class.

Renshi roughly means "polished expert" and is usually given only to teachers with a fifth or sixth dan black belt.

Kyoshi is an "expert teacher" and is awarded to black belts of sixth or seventh degree ranking.

Hanshi is translated as "master" in most texts and is reserved for those of eighth to tenth degree status.

Shihan signifies "a teacher of teachers" and indicates an instructor who has been teaching long enough to have promoted students to instructor status.

Soke means "hereditary head" of a traditional family ryu. Modern karate styles typically don't use this title.

In Korean martial arts, titles are routinely given to all high-ranking black belts. Fifth, sixth, and seventh dan are considered master rankings, while eighth, ninth, and tenth dan are grandmasters.

Sabum is the Korean term for "teacher." Sometimes the honorific "nim" is added to the end *(sabumnim)*.

Shyun is "master."

Saseong is "grandmaster."

Kwan jang nim means roughly the "founder of the school" and signifies the head of a style.

Sensei

The term "sensei" is frequently used in karate magazines and movies. The *kanji* (Chinese characters used in the Japanese writing system) for sensei literally indicate "one who has traveled further down the path." The word denotes wisdom and a mentoring spirit.

In Japan, sensei not only is used by martial arts students to refer to their teachers but is extended to anyone in such a position, so an apprentice would refer to a master artisan as sensei. I agree with Dave Lowry that a sensei is not a therapist.[5] While the goal of a martial arts teacher

Sensei

is to make people healthier both physically and psychologically, she cannot repair a badly damaged person. If a student displays serious personal problems, it is the sensei's responsibility to show him the door. This requires leadership.

So a dojo sensei is a teacher, a leader, and a model for proper technique and application of such.

Is It Legit?

Legitimate certification in the martial arts has long been a bone of contention. A myth long believed by the general public is that an Asian master must certify an instructor before she is considered legitimate. That might have been true in the 1950s, but the rapid expansion of karate and tae kwon do in America has drastically changed the landscape. The United States now has more qualified American-born masters than masters who are Asian nationals.

Still, some people study the martial arts for only a few years and then open their own schools, magically promoting themselves to "master" status. As I've mentioned, there is no one governing body for any martial art. There are, however, both large and small organizations for tae kwon do, karate, kung fu, aikido, etc. Almost any group run by legitimately trained instructors will establish some kind of quality control. The best way to determine the legitimacy of a particular school or instructor is to contact the organization supposedly certifying the black belt and inquire about the instructor's qualifications, including how long he has been teaching. Of course, you should also talk to the instructor personally and find out if he is the kind of person you feel comfortable learning from. Don't forget to speak to the students and parents to get their impressions, and it wouldn't be a bad idea to check with the Better Business Bureau.

Many instructors have started their own systems of American karate or tae kwon do. With regard to determining whether a particular style of martial arts is legitimate, it is necessary to ask, "How long has the instructor been studying?" Most legitimate masters would say that at least fifteen years as a black belt are necessary to have the experience to form one's own system.

The Martial Arts Sourcebook by John Corcoran is a massive and complete reference text to the martial arts of the world.[6] It lists recognized styles of American karate and tae kwon do (along with many other systems like ju-jutsu and kung fu). I'm going to take a risk and list just some of the styles that Corcoran mentions in his book. I've included the ones with which I am familiar—although that is not to say that there are not more that could be considered legitimate.

Recognized Styles of American Karate and Their Founders:

American Freestyle Karate, Dan Anderson

American Goju, Peter Urban

American Karate Systems, Ernest Lieb

American Kenpo, Ed Parker

Bushidokan, Jim Harrison

Cerio Kenpo, Nick Cerio

Hawaiian Kenpo, Bill Ryusaki

Kajukenbo, Adriano Emperado

Keichu Do, Karl Marx

Shin Toshi, Mickey Fisher

Ukidokan, Benny Urquidez

Wado Ki Kai, John Pereira

Won Hop Keun Do, Al Dacascos

Recognized Styles of American Tae Kwon Do
(Or Systems Claiming a Korean Base) **and Their Founders:**

Chayon-Ryu, Kim Soo

Choi Kwang Do, Kwang Jo Choi

Chun Kuk Do, Chuck Norris

Jhoon Rhee Tae Kwon Do, Jhoon Rhee

Jung Su Won, Tae Yun Kim

Pa Sa Ryu, Kang Rhee

Nam Seo Kwan Tae Kwon Do, Keith D. Yates

Song Ahm Tae Kwon Do, Haeung Ung Lee

Profile: J. PAT BURLESON

J. Pat Burleson began his martial arts training in 1957 while stationed in Iwakuni, Japan, with the U.S. Navy. Already a champion boxer, he found the additional kicking techniques of karate fascinating. He won the very first U.S. National Championships in Washington, D.C., in 1964 and earned the nickname of the "granddaddy" of American sport karate.

He went on to become one of the winningest fighters of that early rough and tumble era. Mr. Burleson was one of the pioneers of the martial arts not only in his native Fort Worth, Texas, but also across the country.

He is in several Halls of Fame and has appeared on numerous magazine covers. Now a tenth degree black belt, Mr. Burleson continues to train and teach all around the world. In fact, he teaches more than just martial arts these days, doing seminars for business leaders on his philosophy of "Preparation, Attitude, and Tenacity." These are characteristics that he believes lead to success in business and in life.

See www.karateusa.com.

Dojo Rules

Bow upon first entering and upon the last exit of the workout area.

Do not enter a class late without acknowledgment of instructor (remain in doorway until the instructor bows you in). Note: coming into class late shows disrespect for others, and penalty push-ups may be assigned to students arriving late.

Bow to black belt instructors.

If you arrive early, use the time to stretch and prepare for class. Running and playing is *not* preparation for class.

When called into formation—*run.* Lining up should not take more than thirty seconds.

Seek permission to leave class early (or to go to the restroom).

Always address brown and black belts as "Sir," "Ma'am," "Mr.," etc., rather than "yeah" or "uh-huh."

Actually, all kids should address all adults as "Sir," etc. It is never too early to learn to respect your elders.

Never pass between an instructor and the students (especially if the teacher is speaking to said students), as this is a sign of disrespect. Walk behind the other students instead.

Maintain eye contact with the instructors when they are talking to you. Do not let your attention wander to another group or activity.

When the instructor speaks to the entire group, *all* activity should stop.

After being directly addressed by a black belt, bow in acknowledgment.

Observe quietly and sit in proper position (legs crossed) while others spar.

Do not ask a black belt to spar. This is considered a sign of disrespect.

Do not ask to be promoted. This is a clear indication of wrong motives.

Even outside of class, conduct yourself like a representative of the martial arts. For example, always show self-control and try to avoid fighting or showing off.

Accept responsibility for your own actions. Do not let your ego control you.

A martial artist can only perform at peak efficiency by avoiding drugs and alcohol.

Profile: BILL WALLACE

"Superfoot" Bill Wallace earned his nickname by being one of the sport's fastest kickers (his leg has been clocked in excess of sixty miles per hour). He won twenty-three straight kickboxing title matches, retiring as the undefeated Professional Karate Association (PKA) middleweight world champ.

Born in Portland, Indiana, and originally a judo student, Wallace transitioned to karate after suffering a leg injury in a judo match. Because of that accident, he didn't use his right leg in his karate career, but no one could stop his left leg. He won every major title in point karate before moving into kickboxing. *Black Belt* magazine named him "Competitor of the Year" twice and "Man of the Year" once. He was a close friend and training partner of Elvis Presley.

Mr. Wallace got his nickname after his manager saw an ad for a "Super Foot Long Hot Dog." A professional educator, Mr. Wallace earned a master's degree in kinesiology from Memphis State University and travels widely teaching his fighting style with his unique sense of humor.

See www.superfoot.com.

Common Martial Arts Phrases and Their Translations

Japanese martial arts are the best.

I do Japanese martial arts.

High kicks aren't very effective.

I can't do high kicks.

Sparring is vitally important.

I'm a good fighter, but I can't do much else.

Forms are useless.

Bruce Lee said it, so it must be true, and I'm not very good at them anyway.

I hate martial arts politics.

None of the large organizations recognize me.

Tournaments are a waste of time.

I never won any tournaments.

Our style is the best.

I don't know much about other styles.

Grades aren't important.

I never made very good grades.

He's a good teacher.

He's in my organization.

He's a crummy teacher.

He used to be in my organization, but he split away, and now I don't get any money from him.

I'm "Master" so-and-so.

No one else will call me master, so I have to do it myself.

My instructor is a world champ.

He won the "World Championships" in an elementary school gym in a suburb of Peoria.

I can defend myself against practically anyone.

I can do my kickboxing aerobics routine for an hour straight.

You must be committed to go all the way to black belt.

Our black belt program is the most expensive one we sell.

I'm in the Intergalactic Martial Arts Hall of Fame.

I made up the Intergalactic Martial Arts Hall of Fame and made myself the first inductee.

Korean martial arts are the best.

I do Korean martial arts.

I have collected these over a number of years from several sources. They are funny because they are so true!

Questions from Chapter Three

- What is the Japanese name for uniform?
- Who invented the colored belt rank system?
- What are the seven general levels of rank?
- What should a student do after being addressed by a black belt?
- Should you bow to a brown or red belt?
- What is the Korean word for school? What does it literally mean?
- Is there any single certifying organization for tae kwon do or karate?
- What are the three "Ks" of karate training?
- What is the Japanese word for first degree black belt?
- What does sensei mean?
- What is the Korean term for head of the school?
- Name a couple of recognized styles of American karate.
- Name a couple of recognized styles of American tae kwon do.

Profile: TROY DORSEY

As of this writing, Troy Dorsey is still the only man to ever hold legitimate world titles in karate, kickboxing, and boxing. He won the NABF championship in 1989 (in a bout with Harold Rhodes that the USA Network called the match of the year), the IBF title in 1991, and the IBO crown in 1996. And these were just his boxing championships.

In the martial arts world, he was one of the winningest fighters ever. Perhaps the highlight was in London in 1985—he won both the WAKO point karate and kickboxing titles at the same event. He also held championships from all the major kickboxing associations of his day, including the ISKA and the PKO. He holds records for the fastest kickboxing knockout (nine seconds into the bout) and the most punches in a boxing match (1,527 in a twelve-round fight). Mr. Dorsey was the *Tae Kwon Do Times* "Fighter of the Year" in 1990. He won the same honor given by *Martial Arts Digest* in 2002. He is in numerous martial arts Halls of Fame.

Mr. Dorsey is the oldest of three brothers and actually started his karate training at the age of ten. He now thoroughly enjoys teaching children and adults at his commercial dojos in Texas.

See www.troydorsey.com.

FOUR

Physical Aspects

Although the martial arts stress the development of mind, body, and spirit, most people think of body first. In this chapter I'll give you a brief introduction to the physical aspects of karate and tae kwon do training.

In order to effectively perform a physical activity like karate, your body needs to be in shape. Yes, I know you took up karate or tae kwon do in order to get into shape, but you really need more than one or two classes a week to get in condition. In addition to working out in your karate or tae kwon do class, it is also important to practice on your own several times a week, not just to maintain physical fitness but also to help your body "remember" the physical movements you learned in class.

Fitness, as defined by the experts, consists of three elements: flexibility, muscular strength, and cardiovascular endurance. Martial arts training can give you all three. That's why a karate or tae kwon do class always begins with an exercise period.

Warm-ups and Stretching

Whether you are beginning a formal class or just working out at home, you should always start your physical activity with warm-ups, initial exercises during which the body temperature actually rises. Blood flow increases through muscle tissue, and the body begins to sweat. Warm-ups make your muscles more pliable and more resistant to injury. These factors enable your body to perform at a higher level of efficiency.

A proper warm-up helps to prevent muscle injury and reduces the chance of soreness afterward. A thorough but not exhausting warm-up is what you are aiming for—because you still have your techniques to practice after warming up.

Jumping jacks are a common way to get the blood flowing. Many instructors will warm up by doing the actual activity in slow motion. For example, blocks and kata can be performed extremely slowly, concentrating on getting low balances and performing the moves correctly. Watch (or participate in) an aerobics class for more good warm-up exercises.

Stretching also should be a part of any martial arts workout. Stretches increase your muscle flexibility, which is vital for karate and tae kwon do skills. Actually, stretching exercises do not stretch muscles but the connective tissue (fibers and tendons) that attach the muscles to the bone. The word muscle comes from the Latin for "mouse." Like a mouse, the muscle has a tail (the tendon) that attaches to the bone. Muscles are the motors that move all the parts of your body. It's important to keep them flexible and strong.

Everyone has a different degree of flexibility. Not all youngsters are automatically limber and not all middle-aged students are stiff. You might even be flexible in one part of your body but not in another. Because of these differences, I cannot really put a specific stretching routine into this book and expect that it will work for everyone. So I have only included a very few exercises and must depend on you to listen to your teacher.

Having said that, a good stretching routine usually is divided into a couple of categories: static stretches, or slow-motion movements that are held for a period of time; and dynamic stretches, or swinging motions covering a dynamic range of movement.

While the "bouncing" or "ballistic" stretches are often used in martial arts classes, they can be dangerous because they are hard to control. Static stretches are safer, especially for beginners. A regular routine of these low and deliberate stretches held for about twenty seconds at a time will greatly increase your flexibility.

A stretching program must be performed more than once or twice a week to see results. Each time, try to push yourself a little further; you should experience a certain amount of discomfort but not pain. If you injure yourself by pushing too far, it will mean you have to take time off from your training program to allow the muscle injury to heal.

As you can see, I have provided some examples of stretches. The sitting exercise routine is good for increasing flexibility in your hamstrings (some of the most commonly injured muscles). It is important to keep your knees flat and your legs straight. As in all static stretches, you should not bounce up and down but just slowly pull and hold your position. Do this every day. If you don't go to karate class every day, you can even perform this sitting routine while you sit in front of the television. The important thing is to make stretching a habit. Otherwise, you will never have the high kicks you desire.

Static Sitting Routine

Warm up first.

Start by stretching both feet out to the sides (Figure 4-1). Reach and touch your toes. Hold for about twenty seconds.

Now reach out to each side and hold the stretch to each foot for twenty seconds or so (Figure 4-2).

Put your feet together and grasp firmly as you pull your heels toward your groin (Figure 4-3). This is great for stretching the groin muscles. Be sure to sit straight and do it slowly.

Figure 4-1

Figure 4-2

Figure 4-3

Figure 4-4

Lie flat on your back and stretch one leg at a time toward the ceiling (Figure 4-4). Try to keep the knee from bending, and keep your back flat on the floor.

Dynamic Routine

Dynamic stretches should be done only when you are sufficiently warmed up. Swinging your leg up to the front and side mimics the range of motion you'll do with the snapping kicks (Figure 4-5). Start with a few low swings and graduate to more dynamic movements. These should be controlled motions, so don't swing your leg up violently.

Partner Routine

The advantage of a two-person stretching exercise is that your partner can stretch you a little further than you could by yourself (Figure 4-6). Don't push too far. Stretch slowly and inch by inch. Have your partner push your foot very slowly until you "tap out" with a word or a hand slap.

Figure 4-5

Stretching No-Nos

Remember to warm up. Many experts like to stretch at the end of their workout when the muscles have plenty of blood flow. Of course, martial artists like to stretch out before the main workout because that workout will include kicking techniques. That means spend a few minutes warming up first. By the way, the warm-up should be targeted at the muscles you

Figure 4-6

intend to stretch. If you are going to stretch your hamstrings, for example, do warm-ups to get blood into those leg muscles. We do jumping jacks and sometimes even jogging in place.

Something else to be aware of when practicing stretching routines is to not overextend. That means don't lock your joints out and don't "bounce" into the stretch. If you feel pain (not just discomfort), then you are going too far. You can hold the stretch for ten to twenty seconds at the point of discomfort and then exhale and relax. Trying to maintain the stretch for thirty seconds or more will not give you any increased benefits.

Strength Exercises

Muscular strength is the second component of overall fitness. You can do many exercises to increase strength. The most common are simple sit-ups and push-ups.

Start your strength program slowly, with only ten or fifteen sit-ups or push-ups at a time, and progress to where you can do forty or fifty. Sit-ups produce strong abdominal muscles to help keep your spine straight and thus relieve back stress. Martial artists also want strong stomachs in case they are accidentally hit in the abdomen.

Correct sit-ups (usually called "crunches") should not go any farther than demonstrated in Figure 4-7 and Figure 4-8. Sitting all the way up actually works against the abdominal muscle group and can cause

Figure 4-7

Figure 4-8

Figure 4-9

Figure 4-10

lower back soreness. Exhale as you curl your body up, and hold it a second or two in the crunch position.

Although many martial arts classes do knuckle push-ups, I wouldn't recommend that you do more than twenty-five or so at one time because of the stress on your knuckles and wrists. If you really can do fifty or a hundred push-ups at once (as a lot of people can), do "regulation" push-ups on your palms. Keep your hands under the shoulders.

Figure 4-11

Martial arts push-ups are performed with fists tight and the first two knuckles making contact with the floor (Figure 4-9 to 4-10). This strengthens not only the arms and shoulders but the wrists as well. It also gets you used to pointing the knuckles for punches.

Years ago, some instructors said weight training was bad for martial artists because it was thought bulky muscles would slow you down. Today, however, most teachers recommend a weight program for strength and stamina. You should consult a personal trainer or a specialist at a health club or gym before starting a rigorous program, especially if you are out of shape to begin with. The latest research shows that weight training is excellent for women (who are at greater risk of osteoporosis) and even benefits older people. So go ahead and hit the weights (Figure 4-11).

Endurance Exercises

As the third part of your fitness program, you should build in some endurance exercises. These activities can be as simple as walking, jogging, riding a bike, or swimming. You can also increase your cardiovascular capabilities by doing your karate moves. Try performing a number of forms over and over again. Hitting a training bag with kicks and punches (bag gloves are recommended) also does wonders for your endurance.

My friends at the Cooper Institute for Aerobic Research tell me that exercise that is continuous for at least twelve to fifteen minutes increases your fitness level much more than a start and stop exercise routine. That means you must do forms or spar for an extended period of time rather than just a minute or two followed by rest.[1]

The important thing to remember in doing cardiovascular exercise is that you want to get your heart rate elevated past your normal rate for that twelve to fifteen minute period. That means you need to check your heart rate during exercise, and you have to know what the normal rate for your age group is. (See the chart on page 90.)

Remember that the point of "aerobic" exercise is that it has to be continuous and steady. Aerobic means requiring air or, more specifically, oxygen. Your muscles use oxygen to work, and their need for oxygen increases as you exercise. As your need for oxygen goes up, so does your heart rate. That's why the heart rate chart is a good measure of how hard your muscles are working.

If you do an aerobic exercise like karate or tae kwon do for that magic twelve to fifteen minutes at a time, it will lead to better endurance and firmer muscles with less "fat marbling."

Remember that any exercise, from walking to free-sparring, requires a "warm-up" period to get your heart rate into the target zone. That can vary from two to five minutes, so don't start your fifteen minute countdown until after the first few minutes.

According to studies on the aerobic benefits of certain types of exercises, martial arts fall somewhere in the middle. Of course, a vigorous ten minute sparring match against a champion black belt is going to be a lot more of a cardiovascular workout than a few kicks and punches and some medium power forms. So use common sense when trying to measure your martial arts workouts for fitness.

For most martial artists, fitness is a side benefit of training—not the main purpose. When I teach or practice in a tae kwon do class, I'm usually concentrating on perfecting techniques or learning new moves rather than developing a higher fitness level. For this reason, I think you are probably better off doing a continuous aerobic exercise like jogging or swimming for your endurance levels and practicing martial arts for developing specific skills—and, of course, for fun.

> *Exercise is the best way to control your stress, gain overall health benefits, and control your weight.*
>
> —Dr. Kenneth Cooper, "Father of Aerobics"

How to Read an Aerobic Benefit Chart

You want to get your heart rate into the target zone for your age for approximately twelve to fifteen minutes to increase your cardiovascular fitness level. For example, if you are thirty years old, your target rate is between 132 and 152 heartbeats per minute. Immediately after exercising, take your pulse on either your wrist or the carotid artery (alongside the Adam's apple). Count the beats for ten seconds and multiply by six to figure your beats per minute. Note that your heart starts to slow down immediately after you stop running, cycling, etc., so if you wait even a few seconds your count will be off.

Dr. Kenneth Cooper

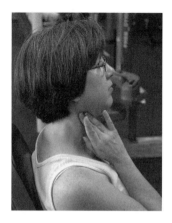

Checking the heart rate

Age	Target heart rate (between 12 and 15 minutes)
20	140 to 160
25	136 to 156
30	132 to 152
35	129 to 149
40	125 to 145
45	121 to 141
50	117 to 137
55	114 to 134
60	110 to 130

Estimated Calories Burned per Minute by Weight
(Assuming at least twelve minutes of activity)

	130 lb. person	150 lb. person	170 lb. person
Cycling	3.8	4.4	4.9
Walking	4.7	5.4	6.2
Dancing	6.1	7.0	7.9
Karate forms	6.5	7.2	8.1
Sparring	7.5	8.2	9.1
Running	8.0	9.2	10.5
Basketball	8.1	9.4	10.6
Swimming	9.2	10.6	12.0

Balances and Stances

Stances are the first karate or tae kwon do skill you must learn; they are the foundation of everything else to come. Without a good stance, you can't effectively punch, kick, or block.

Figure 4-14   **Figure 4-15**

Because no single stance will be effective in all situations, it's important to learn several. It is not the purpose of this book to show you any more than a few basic stances, so you need to rely on your teacher for complete instruction.

The ready stance (*chunbi* in Korean, *hachiji-dachi* in Japanese) is the typical classroom stance (Figure 4-14). The students assume it whenever they are receiving instructions from the teacher. It is also the beginning and end of most martial arts patterns. The feet are parallel, with the weight exactly centered. The fists are held slightly in front of the body with front knuckles pointing toward each other. The arms should be slightly rounded.

The forward or front stance (*chongul-sogi* or *ap-sogi* in Korean, *zenkutsu-dachi* in Japanese) is quite stable (Figure 4-15). The front leg is bent so that the lower part of the leg is straight up and down, perpen-

Figure 4-16   Figure 4-17

dicular to the floor. The rear leg is extended straight back so that your body is supported if someone pushes you from the front. Note that the heel of the front foot and the toe of the rear foot are at the corners of a square approximately one shoulder-width.

The back stance (*fugil-sogi* in Korean, *kokutsu-dachi* in Japanese) may not be as stable as the front stance, but it is definitely more mobile (Figure 4-16). Both legs are bent for quick motions; however, most of the weight rests over the rear foot, so you can quickly lift the front leg for a kick. Note that the heels line up on an even line, and 60 percent to 70 percent of the weight is on the back foot, although you can easily shift forward and backward in this stance.

The "karate walk" is usually done in a forward balance (Figure 4-17). By sliding the foot in a slight inward direction when stepping forward, your head level remains the same, reducing the up-and-down motion that can signal movement to an opponent. The center of gravity also stays even, meaning that you are less likely to be caught off-balance if interrupted in the middle of a step.

Turning—The About-Face

When in forward stance (Figure 4-18), the about-face (*twi-tura* in Korean, *mawate* in Japanese) is done by crossing the back leg in a straight line. Once the proper distance has been established, rotate your body until you are facing the opposite direction in a good forward stance.

In back balance (Figure 4-19), merely lift your toes and pivot on your heels until you face the opposite direction. Note that the heels remain on the same line. When turning in either forward or back balance, be sure to keep your hands up, so you don't turn into a punch or other attack.

Figure 4-18   Figure 4-19

Other Stances

The horse stance (*kima-sogi* in Korean, *kiba-dachi* in Japanese) is sometimes also called a straddle stance (Figure 4-20). The feet are parallel and about one-and-a-half to two shoulder-widths apart. Tense the

Figure 4-20   Figure 4-21

abdominal muscles and bring your pelvis forward to attain a straight spine and low center of gravity. The horse stance is often used for practice punching.

The cat stance (*twitpal-sogi* in Korean, *nekoahi-dachi* in Japanese) is specifically designed to allow you to kick with the front leg with little or no rocking motion to the rear (Figure 4-21). This balance resembles the back stance except the front foot is pulled off the floor with only the ball of the foot touching.

Stability

Stability is a basic concept in karate and tae kwon do. Stability is your ability to stand up and not get knocked over when blocking or striking. Your stability is closely related to your center of gravity. Your center of gravity is, in turn, affected by how you stand. Therefore, it is critically important that you understand the purpose and function of each of your karate balances.

Here are three things to remember.

Figure 4-22. Your center of gravity must fall within your base of support if you are to remain stable. That is, if you lean too far one way or the other, you'll be in danger of falling down. In this illustration the dotted line indicates your center of gravity (mid-hip).

Of course, the wider your base of support, the easier it is to keep your center over it. Therefore, a wide stance is more stable than a narrow stance. A problem arises when you kick, however, because now your base of support is extremely narrow: just one foot on the ground. That is why you must not lean too far when kicking, and why you must return the kicking foot back to the ground quickly to regain your stability.

Figure 4-22   Figure 4-23

Both of these kicks are off-balance because the center of gravity (dotted line) is not over the supporting foot.

Figure 4-23. The lower you are, the more stable you are; just spread your feet a little to increase stability. Obviously, you can't stay in a very low stance during the entire duration of a fight. Sometimes you have to move fast, which means you must raise your center. Remember that when you hit your opponent, you don't want to have a high and unstable center. Spread your legs and drop your hips when you strike, especially with hand techniques (see below.)

Figure 4-24. Finally, the heavier you are, the more stable you are. I'm not telling you to gain weight to become a better martial artist. I am, however, warning you that a bigger opponent is going to be much harder for you to push around than a smaller one. If you do encounter a much larger attacker, you must use your inherent advantages, which will, hopefully, be quickness and "street smarts."

Figure 4-24

Targets

I often tell my students that karate or tae kwon do doesn't make you Superman. It merely teaches you how to hit and where to hit. Common target points—where to hit—can be classified into two main divisions. The primary targets—the places where you can very easily hurt someone—are the eyes, throat, and groin. These are the first areas to target in a self-defense situation. The secondary targets—places where it takes a little more force to hurt an attacker, but where he will nevertheless feel a well-placed strike—are the temple, bridge of the nose, collarbone, solar plexus, ribs, neck (side and back), kidney, knee, shin, and instep.

I can't overemphasize the importance of hitting an attacker right on the proper target. You could execute a fairly good karate punch or kick, but if you hit her in the shoulder or hipbone, you will only make her mad. Your techniques are only as effective as the targets you throw them to. This is one of the primary points to learn in self-defense training.

There are also many "pressure points" or vital areas on the human body. It is too complicated a topic to go into here, but there are a lot good books on the subject, many of which are listed in the back of this book.

Striking Techniques

A basic premise of the martial arts is that you can do damage to an attacker by using your own body as a weapon. Of course, you have to hit the opponent in the right place. Most schools of American karate and tae kwon do utilize nine body parts as weapons—hands, feet, elbows, knees, and head.

It takes diligent practice to perfect each of these blows. Positioning of the feet and the amount of body twist have as much to do with the technique's effectiveness as do muscle power and speed. You simply

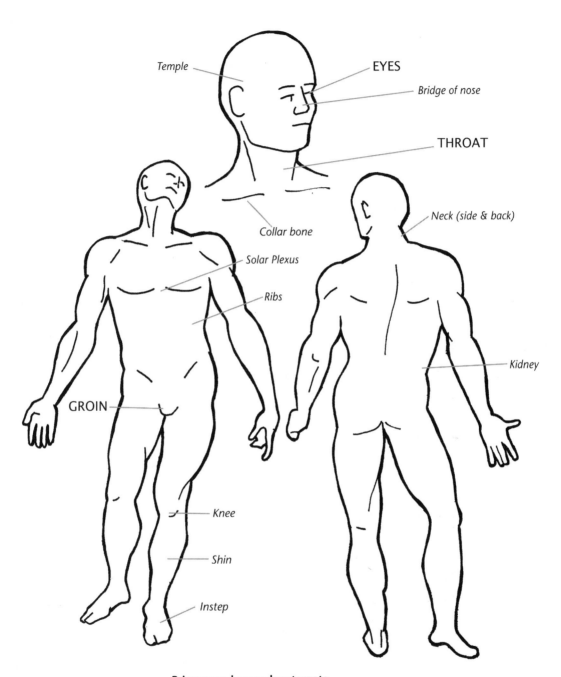

Temple

EYES

Bridge of nose

THROAT

Collar bone

Neck (side & back)

Solar Plexus

Ribs

Kidney

GROIN

Knee

Shin

Instep

Primary and secondary targets

can't learn karate or tae kwon do techniques from a book—spend time in the classroom with your instructor.

Figure 4-26 Punch

Figure 4-27 Knife-hand

Hands

The most commonly used hand technique is the closed-fist punch (*jirgi* in Korean, *zuki* in Japanese). To make a fist, curl the fingers tightly and tuck the thumb in (Figure 4-26).

The striking surface is the first two knuckles. Be sure and keep the wrist straight, so it won't collapse on impact.

Many people believe the chop is used more frequently than it really is—probably because television and movie martial artists seem to be always using it. Wearing padded gloves in sport competition has reduced the frequency of the knife-hand, although the classic chop is still a valuable weapon for self-defense.

To form a knife-hand (*sudo* in Korean, *shuto* in Japanese), keep your fingers together and flex them slightly (Figure 4-27). The thumb should be bent and not extended away from the hand. As with the punch, keep your wrist straight. The striking surface is slightly to

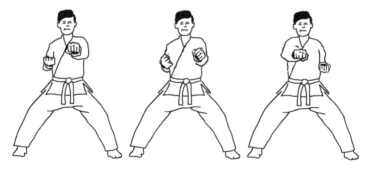

Figure 4-28 Twisting the punch

the palm side of the hand so contact with the bony edge is reduced.

A twisting punch will be a new concept to someone not familiar with the martial arts. The karate punch rotates as it extends. Note the right fist in Figure 4-28 is palm up at the hip. As the punch begins to travel out, it turns until the arm is extended and the fist is palm-side down. This twisting helps to keep the punch on target and increases power. The example I often use is the rotation of a bullet coming out of a gun.

Figure 4-29 Don't bend the wrist

A common mistake is not keeping the wrist straight when striking with a punch. A bent wrist can buckle on impact and cause injury.

The first two knuckles should be the main striking surface of a closed fist punch. They are the largest and strongest knuckles. Your last knuckle (the "pinkie") is the smallest and weakest, and it is subject to injury if you allow it to protrude and hit a hard target (like a board).

Figure 4-30 Protect the "pinkie" knuckle

The front hand punch is called a jab. It's a quick technique that is hard to block if you snap your hand. Snap also increases power in the blow, which is something you need with this strike because there is less hip motion than with a reverse punch.

Figure 4-31 Jab

Figure 4-32 Reverse punch

Figure 4-33   Figure 4-34   Figure 4-35

The reverse punch (*bandae jirugi* in Korean, *gaku-zuki* in Japanese), which uses the back or "reverse" hand, is a more common punch in karate and tae kwon do. Because this punch is so frequently used, you should spend some time learning its finer points. The reverse punch uses a twist of the hips to generate more power than the jab. The only drawback to this technique is that you are momentarily open for a counterstrike if you execute the reverse punch too slowly.

The reverse punch can be executed with the palm down—as in Figure 4-33, which shows a punch to the head. Or the reverse punch can be executed palm up—as in Figure 4-34, which depicts an inverted punch to the solar plexus. In both cases the hips twist for maximum power.

Whether you punch low or high, you should either grab or block with your front hand while you reverse punch with the rear fist (Figure 4-35). If you do not keep your front hand up, you might get a nasty surprise from a fast opponent.

For maximum speed and impact, imagine your hips are "wound-up" like a toy airplane propeller (Figure 4-36). The rubber band is wound tightly, and when you let go there is an explosion of torque and motion into the punch.

Figure 4-36

Body Movement

You should use your whole body for a punch (or any hand strike). This gives you maximum power as well as an extended reach. Note that in all these photos the distance between the feet stays the same. Figure 4-37 shows normal fighting distance. In Figure 4-38, I shoot out a jab, but the blow falls short.

However, by simply using my body, I am able to make contact with my opponent's face (Figure 4-39). (If I lean too far forward, I'll lose my balance!)

Figure 4-37   Figure 4-38   Figure 4-39

Figure 4-40. You can close the gap between you and your opponent by twisting your hips. If you understand this principle and he does not, you can easily punch a much larger person.

Figure 4-40

More Hand Techniques

The backfist (Figure 4-41) is a technique that hits with the back of the knuckles rather than the front surface, as in a jab. It is good for a quick surprise strike because of its speed and the close proximity of the hand

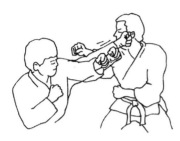

Figure 4-41

Figure 4-42

Figure 4-43

Figure 4-44

to the target (usually the temple or nose area.) Like the jab, you must snap the fist back to get the concussive effect and maximize power.

Figure 4-42. The ridgehand is sometimes called a reverse chop because you hit with the opposite side of the open hand. It is especially good for striking the neck or throat areas. The angle of attack makes the ridgehand more difficult to block than a straight-line technique.

A ridgehand should start in a straight line and not hook until the last second (Figure 4-43). This final hooking motion enables the ridgehand to wrap around an opponent's block. The striking surface is the index knuckle on the side of the hand (Figure 4-44).

Figure 4-45. The palm heel is a great self-defense technique. It is also good for women and children, who may not have large hands and knuckles. Strike with the base of the palm while pulling your fingers back out of the way.

Figure 4-46. The hammer fist is a good technique to use to break your first board. Because you hit with the side of the fist, you are less likely to hurt your knuckles as with a punch. Because the fingers are tucked into a fist, you are not as likely to hit your little finger on the board as with a chop. Don't stop at the surface of the board, but drive your hammer fist *past* the board. Don't forget to yell, either!

Figure 4-45   Figure 4-46

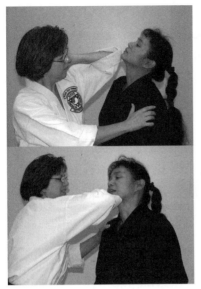

Figure 4-47

Figure 4-48

Figure 4-49

Other weapons

You also have elbows, knees, and even your head on the list of bodily weapons.

An elbow can travel in several different directions. Do not hit with the tip of the bone but with the flat part of the arm near the elbow point. Elbows are banned in competitions because they can be so devastating. Of course, that's what makes them so good for self-defense (Figure 4-47). The elbow can be used rising to the chin or swinging sideways to face or head.

Figure 4-50

Figure 4-48. You can drive an elbow to the rear or come downward on an opponent's neck or spine.

Figure 4-49. A rising knee to the groin is the best defense for those in-close grabs.

Figure 4-50. A head butt can be very effective if someone is very close and you cannot use your hands or feet. However, you must be sure to hit with the upper forehead (along the hairline) and not with your face!

We'll cover more complete uses of all these techniques in the chapter on self-defense.

Kicking Techniques

These are the techniques that every would-be tae kwon do expert imagines himself or herself doing. Indeed, kicks are what make karate and tae kwon do different from boxing or other kinds of fighting that just use the hands.

Figure 4-51

Figure 4-52   Wrong / Right

Your legs are not only stronger than your arms but longer, so it stands to reason that a kick is a more effective blow than a punch. However, the legs have several disadvantages in comparison to hand strikes. First, the feet are usually slower than the hands. Also, because most people don't use their legs in everyday activities (like they do with arms and hands), kicks are initially awkward and take much, much more practice to execute correctly. Finally, because you end up standing on just one leg (or even none in a jumping kick), balance becomes much more critical than with a simple punch.

Figure 4-51. The leg is longer than the arm. That's how a smaller person can effectively kick a larger person and still stay out of range of a punch or grab.

Figure 4-52. Wrong way: Center of balance (see dotted line) is too far back. Arms are down too low to block. Head is down too low to see. Right way: Center of balance is over the center of the supporting foot (see dotted line). Head and hands are up. Hips are thrust out to give more weight to the kick.

Kicking Dos and Don'ts

To stay balanced, your center of gravity must stay within your base of support. In other words, if you lean too far one way or the other, you'll be pushed off balance when you make contact. Here are a few other points to keep in mind when attempting to kick an attacker.

1. Keep your eyes on your opponent. If you look away as you kick, you're likely to miss. (This is a common mistake with beginners.)
2. Don't use just the weight of your leg; move your whole body and hips into the kick. This increases momentum and puts everything you've got behind it.
3. Snap the foot back immediately to keep it from being grabbed.
4. Your fold should not give away your imminent attack. That means don't swing or lift your arms before you kick. Don't lean over or twist your body until the kick is on its way. If you raise your arms and lean back before you even start to kick, I can guarantee your opponent will be able to avoid or block the kick.
5. Keep your hands up when you kick. After all, you are kicking your opponent in the first place because she is trying to hit you! It would be foolish to keep your hands at your side when someone is attempting to break your nose.

The Basic Kicks

Figures 4-53 to 4-55. To execute a front kick (*ap-chagi* in Korean, *mae-geri* in Japanese), raise the kicking foot up to knee level. Snap the foot out, striking with the ball of the foot. Note the slight hip thrust to gain distance and power. Immediately snap the foot back to the knee.

Figure 4-53

Figure 4-54

Figure 4-55

Figure 4-56

Figure 4-56. You also can strike with the instep of the foot. This applies to a self-defense situation in which you probably would be wearing shoes and will be kicking between an assailant's legs.

Figures 4-57 to 4-59. To execute a side kick (*yop-chagi* in Korean, *yoko-geri* in Japanese), raise the foot to knee level. Note how high the knee of the kicking leg is folded. Strike with the heel of the foot. Snap the foot back.

Figure 4-57

Figure 4-58

Figure 4-59

Figure 4-60   Figure 4-61   Figure 4-62

Figure 4-60. In many Okinawan and Japanese systems of karate, the preferred striking surface is the edge, or blade, of the foot.

The fighters in Figure 4-61 are too close. You'll need some room to throw a side kick (although experienced fighters can hit you with a kick when you least expect it). Figure 4-62 depicts proper distance. A side kick has to be timed just right. You might want to practice on a kicking bag to figure out the proper distance for you.

Figures 4-63 to 4-66 show the execution of a roundhouse kick (*tolyo-chagi* in Korean, *mawashi-geri* in Japanese). A typical roundhouse kick starts in a back balance or fighting stance. Twist the body, bringing the

Figure 4-63   Figure 4-64   Figure 4-65   Figure 4-66

Figure 4-67   Figure 4-68   Figure 4-69

kicking leg up high, and point the knee toward your target. Snap the kick out, striking with either the ball of the foot (shown) or the instep. Immediately snap the foot back, keeping the knee up.

Figures 4-67 to 4-69. When executing a back kick (*dwi-chagi* in Korean, *ushiro-geri* in Japanese), as with a front kick, the fold is knee-high. Striking surface is the heel.

Figures 4-70 to 4-72. As the name implies, the hooking heel kick (*huryo-chagi* in Korean, *kakato-geri* in Japanese) hooks back into the target, striking with the back of your heel.

Figures 4-73 to 4-75. The crescent kick (*pyojuk-chagi* in Korean, *mika-*

Figure 4-70   Figure 4-71   Figure 4-72

Figure 4-73   Figure 4-74   Figure 4-75

suki-geri in Japanese) begins like a front kick, with the knee raised high. The striking surface is the inside bottom edge of the foot. This kick can be used to knock something out of an attacker's hand.

Figures 4-76 to 4-78. To execute a turning back kick (*twi-tollyo-chagi* in Korean, *ushiro-mawatte-geri* in Japanese), turn your back toward your opponent. Looking over your shoulder, snap the kick out, striking with the heel. Be sure to snap the foot back, so your opponent cannot grab your leg.

Figures 4-79 to 4-81. To execute a double jump front kick (*eadan-ahp-chagi* in Korean, *tobi-mae-geri* in Japanese), begin by executing a

Figure 4-76   Figure 4-77   Figure 4-78

Figure 4-79

Figure 4-80

Figure 4-81

Figure 4-82

Figure 4-83

normal front snap kick. As you bring the kick back, leap off the ground with the opposite foot. Jump forward with the second kick.

The ax kick is depicted in Figure 4-82. A favorite tae kwon do technique is a dropping ax kick. It helps if you're tall.

The classic karate photo is usually the flying side kick (Figure 4-83). Originally, this was thought to have been devised to knock a mounted warrior off a horse. It has less street self-defense application in today's society, but it makes for a great photograph.

Blocking

While your best defense is, of course, avoiding a fight in the first place, sometimes you have to defend yourself with blocking techniques. Because karate and tae kwon do are hard-style "striking" arts, most of the blocks are, in

Figure 4-84   **Figure 4-85**   **Figure 4-86**

essence, defensive strikes used to deflect or stop an attacker's blows.

As with offensive strikes, many parts of your body can be used to perform the techniques. Here are five out of many possible blocking techniques. Not all schools will perform them in this exact manner, but they are similar from style to style.

Figure 4-87   **Figure 4-88**

Figure 4-84 to 4-86. The low block (*hardan-marki* in Korean, *gedan-uke* in Japanese) is used to defend from a strike to the abdomen or groin. Begin by crossing the blocking arm on top. Step out while forcefully dropping the fist. The contact point is the forearm. Pull the opposite hand back to increase body twist and power.

Figure 4-87 to 4-88. The rising block (*chukyo-marki* in Korean, *age-uke* in Japanese), sometimes called a "high" block, or *sangdan-marki* in Korean, deflects a downward strike. Raise the non-blocking arm and

Figure 4-89

Figure 4-90

lower the other fist in front of the groin to protect that area. Step out and swing the forearm up. The fist should be high over the head to deflect the attack.

Figure 4-89 to 4-90. The inside block (*ahn-marki* in Korean, *soto-uke* in Japanese) is sometimes also called a "fore-strike," or *arb-cheegee* in Korean. It is used to defend the face area. Pull the blocking arm behind your head. Step forward and block with the inner forearm. Just before impact, rotate the wrist so the palm turns toward your face.

Figure 4-91 to 4-92. The outside block (*yop-marki* in Korean, *uchi-uke* in Japanese) also defends the face. Fold the blocking arm under the opposite elbow. Step out and block with the outer forearm. The palm should face you when you strike.

Figure 4-91

Figure 4-92

Figure 4-93 to 4-94. The knife-hand block (*sudo-marki* in Korean, *shuto-uke* in Japanese) is a variant of the outside block; it is performed with the open hand, allowing you to grab the opponent's arm. Cross your open hands at the wrists and pull back close to the right shoulder before you step out. Block with the edge of the knife-hand. A last-second wrist rotation adds to the power of this block.

Figure 4-93

Figure 4-94

A Word about Application

Blocking techniques can be described as totally defensive moves or as a combination of defense and offense. An old karate axiom states, "A block is a strike, and a strike is a block." Often an instructor will only explain the simplest applications because she wants the student to concentrate on the memorization of the moment and not get too overwhelmed with complicated theory and principles.

I like to show the more sophisticated elements of each so-called basic block as soon as I think the student is coordinated enough (both physically and mentally) to absorb it. Usually that's not until green or blue belt level.

But let's assume you are ready to see and to comprehend, "Grasshopper." Here are just a few of the possible applications of the basic blocks. There are many, many more applications of these simple movements. In fact there are several good books on the whole topic of *bunkai* (Japanese for "application"). If you are interested in this important topic, I suggest you start researching, both by reading and by seeking out knowledgeable instructors.

Figure 4-95

Figure 4-96

Figure 4-97

Low block application

Figure 4-95. Simple: Block an incoming kick.

Figures 4-96 to 4-97. Advanced: The folding motion is actually the block. The downward movement is a rotation to swing the attacker's arm down and to the side so you can counter strike.

Rising block application

Figure 4-98. Simple: Block an incoming chop.

Figures 4-99 to 4-100. Advanced: Pulling the hand down keeps the opponent from grabbing you. The rising motion can be an upward hammer strike.

Figure 4-98

Figure 4-99

Figure 4-100

Figure 4-101   Figure 4-102   Figure 4-103

Inside block application

Figure 4-101. Simple: Block an incoming punch.

Figures 4-102 to 4-103. Advanced: Pin the attacker's hand as he grabs for your lapel. Move in with an arm break.

Outside block application

Figure 4-104. Simple: Block an incoming punch.

Figures 4-105 to 4-106. Advanced: The folding motion is the block. Then strike with a back fist or with the extended thumb knuckle to a pressure point.

Figure 4-104   Figure 4-105   Figure 4-106

Figure 4-107   **Figure 4-108**   **Figure 4-109**

Knife-hand block application

Figure 4-107. Simple: Block an incoming punch.

Figures 4-108 to 4-109. Advanced: The fold is a block. Then chop to the opponent's neck. Again, I am pulling with the opposite hand.

Profile: LINDA DENLEY

Beginning her martial arts training in Tang Soo Do in 1973, Linda Denley is one of the fiercest karate competitors to ever enter the ring, male or female. She was rated the number one woman fighter from 1973 until 1996, when she finally retired. At one point she went nine years without losing a tournament match. She is in the MARS Hall of Fame, the NASKA Hall of Fame, and the Diamond National Hall of Fame. She was also the first woman ever to be named to the *Black Belt* magazine Hall of Fame, in 1980.

A natural athlete from a large family (twelve kids), Denley qualified for the Olympics in track and field while still in high school in 1976 (she ran the 100-yard dash in a record 10.2 seconds), but was then disqualified because she had already won money on the karate circuit. In 1979 she decided to pass on an opportunity to play semi-professional basketball with the Houston Angels because of her martial arts career. Denley also used to be a professional "swing out" dancer—think *Dancing with the Stars*–type moves. She recently biked in her first two-day MS 150 (a cycling tour to benefit multiple sclerosis) and came in fourth out of more than ten thousand participants!

She has appeared in movies and television shows and still works with her students and other community youth. Jefferson Davis High School in Houston holds a "Linda Denley Day" every year to honor her accomplishments and contributions.

Questions from Chapter Four

■ Why should you warm up before stretching?

■ What are the three components of fitness?

■ How do you take your pulse after exercising to figure out your heart rate?

■ Name the three primary target areas.

■ An old karate saying is "A strike is a _____, a _____ is a strike."

Mike Proctor Sensei

FIVE

Training Patterns

"Forms are the very foundation of the martial arts."
"Forms are useless for real fighting." These are the
two opposite but prevalent views of the training patterns in karate and tae kwon do. Which is correct? To
figure out an answer to that question, we'll have to
look at the history of training forms.

Michael Rosenbaum, in his fascinating book *Kata
and the Transmission of Knowledge,* says that prearranged routines for training evolved from three
basic methods of fighting: military, civilian, and
sport.[1] He classifies military routines as those involv-
ing battlefield weaponry such as spears, swords, and
shields. He points out that civilian karate kata were
less focused on offensive battlefield tactics than on
self-defense. They relied more on empty-hand techniques or weapons such as walking sticks or hand-
held daggers. He also rightly points out that combative sports are not
a modern invention but were common in past cultures—witness
medieval jousting and Japanese sumo wrestling. The evolution of all
three areas, says Rosenbaum, were influenced by their prearranged
patterns of training.

In the early days of civilian karate (and remember, karate really only came into its own in the late nineteenth and early twentieth centuries), practitioners didn't engage in free-sparring, they only did kata.[2] And before the 1880s, each karateka (karate practitioner) only knew and practiced a very few forms. Gichin Funakoshi noted that it was unusual for a master to teach more than a handful of kata. They spent decades practicing various technical applications (bunkai) of a single pattern.

Today it is not unusual for an advanced student to know fifteen to twenty-five kata, as well as a couple of "competition" forms just for tournaments. The prevailing attitude in most modern schools seems to be: "OK, what forms do I have to learn for my next belt?" As far back as the 1960s, Bruce Lee was saying forms weren't very useful in learning how to fight, and champions like Bill Wallace echoed that sentiment in the 1970s.

It wasn't until the 1970s that kata divisions were incorporated into tournaments, and even then those champions weren't held in as high esteem as the fighting champs. I know because I was one of them.

But a funny thing happened over the next few years. Many of those sparring champions dropped out of karate and tae kwon do when they got too old to compete, while the students who practiced their kata tended to stay with their training. They were, it seemed, the real martial artists.

Today there is a movement back to kata and an attempt to understand the meanings behind those patterns. After all, if those old masters found it useful to practice kata repeatedly over the decades, it must have some application, right?

Indeed, kata teaches you valuable and even life-saving techniques—even if some kata steps may look downright weird. Holding both hands over your head and pulling into a cat stance? Come on! That can't be useful when someone is attacking with a jump side kick!

And that is precisely the point. Remember when I said that the early masters did not spar? As Rosenbaum says, their kata techniques were designed for in-close, civilian (we might say "street") self-defense.

Bill Burgar, in his excellent book *Five Years, One Kata*, asks an interesting question. Which are you most likely to be attacked with in a street fight: a jump spin kick, a swinging round punch, or a headlock?

You'll no doubt agree with me that it is the punch first, the grab next, and last—maybe—the jump kick. If that is the case, then traditional kata, designed without sport-type free-sparring in mind, would be constructed to handle those types of in-close attacks.

You can see why those free-sparring champions would say that kata doesn't apply to what they do in the ring, because it really doesn't. But if you want to defend against someone coming up to you, swinging wildly at your face at close range, and trying to grab you and slam you to the ground—then kata techniques are great.

"OK, I get it," you say. But now there's another problem. Most martial arts teachers today don't really understand what the heck those moves are anymore.

Another quick history lesson is in order. As Funakoshi notes in his book *Karate-do Nyumon*, the historical backgrounds and meanings of most kata were almost completely oral (a sometimes unreliable method of preserving truth and meaning). So much of the specifics of kata technique have been passed down from teacher to student, from father to son. That means everything—from who designed the pattern to what exactly it is trying to teach—is subject to misinterpretation and accidental or even intentional forgetfulness (sometimes the master didn't want certain people to know his most secret applications).

And just as kata today are altered by competitors to make themselves look good in a tournament (back flips, anyone?), kata were undoubtedly altered by some old masters to fit their own strengths and weaknesses.

So we find ourselves in a quandary: how do we find the useful self-defense applications of our forms?

The good news is that you don't have to determine exactly what Choson Miyagi meant when he made up a certain form—you just have to be able to come up with a practical application that fits you.

And that can only come with martial arts experience. So we go back to my original thought that a true martial artist will continue studying over a period of years (even decades) and become so adept at a whole repertoire of techniques that kata become a gold mine of new and exciting applications for self-defense.

Performance Training

Kata training can be divided into a number of steps. I am going to suggest three.

Stage one: just learn the sequence. When you are worried about getting the steps out of order, it's hard to work on other elements such as power and balance. If you have to, get a video or a book (hey, like this one!) to help you remember the patterns.

Stage two: work on the specifics. Focus on proper targeting—that means punch to the solar plexus and not the shoulder. Concentrate on correct breathing; don't hold your breath. Note your balances and your body positioning. At this point, you may have to move from learning out of a book to actually working with a competent teacher.

Stage three: perform without thinking. Some call this "moving Zen" or "no mind." It means that your outward performance is secondary to your inward expression of focus and power. That only happens if you relax and let your mind and body work together. I know this is easy to say but hard to do. You'll just have to trust that it will come after much practice. A professional ice skater seems to glide effortlessly across the ice, but it took years to get to that completely relaxed state of grace. You can do it too!

Tips

Forms should begin and end with a bow of respect. It gets you in the proper mental framework, which is especially important for kids who just sail through their kata without focus.

Breathe with each move, but don't huff and puff like a locomotive train. Exhale from the abdomen, and concentrate your energy to the point of impact.

Many beginning students see the power that the black belts generate, and they try to emulate it by straining every muscle in their bodies. The key is to relax and not use too much force because it can slow you down and make you look "robotic."

Visualize an opponent at every turn. After all, you are performing self-defense moves against another person. It helps to imagine someone grabbing or punching at you as you deflect and strike. Funakoshi said, "Your opponent must always be present in your mind."

It also would help if you knew where the target points were. Go back to the chart in chapter four. Realize, too, that sometimes you are striking a pressure point instead of just an anatomical target.

If you let your body just go through the pattern, it will begin to remember how to move. Forms are what some call mnemonic patterns to train muscle memory and to build habits. For example, a bad habit might be to close your eyes and flinch when someone starts to swing at you. A good habit—built by doing a lot of kata—would be to step off-line from the attack and deflect with a raised hand.

A Final Word

The last thing I want to say before we get into the actual forms and their individual steps is that it is not my intent to denigrate free-sparring with my prior comments. Sparring is a valuable part of any martial arts style's curriculum because it teaches things such as distancing and timing. It gets you into physical condition and—sometimes—can even reveal to you what it's like to get hit in the stomach or the face.

I have devoted a whole chapter to free-sparring later on in this book. Still, hopefully, you will see that my emphasis on kata is born out of a belief that in order to defend yourself on a street, you need to know some in-close, time-proven techniques.

> *The use of strength in continuous, rapid motions does not mean one is skilled.*
>
> —Gichin Funakoshi

> *Kata is the language of the martial arts. Each kata is, in a way, a letter in the karate alphabet and one must learn this alphabet before one can build words.*
>
> —Richard Kim

Kata

The Kata

"Kata" is a combination of *kanji* characters (Figure 5-2). The top element means "to make or act." The bottom symbol indicates "the earth," and together the characters literally mean to make a pattern in the earth. Thus the practice of kata is the act of repeating a pattern of movements so that they become ingrained—second nature to you.

The goals of kata have changed from the days when a series of techniques were designed to defend against multiple attacks to one's vulnerable targets and to end said attacks as quickly as possible. Modern karate and tae kwon do forms are often just performance activities in which the techniques are geared toward garnering the highest points from the judges. High kicks, handstands, and backflips are performance enhancers popular in the XMA (extreme martial arts) trend. So modern, sport kata are longer (both in duration and in reach of technique) because that affords more opportunity to show off athletic skill and wow the audience. Traditional kata, by contrast, are composed of shorter moves and are more concise. You have probably guessed that I am a traditionalist.

Okinawan

As we have already covered in the chapter on martial arts history, karate started in Okinawa. It is thought that most of the Okinawa Te kata came directly from Chinese patterns or were developed by Okinawan masters based on their own experience. Two of the oldest Okinawan systems were Shorin-ryu and Shorei-ryu. There are several branches of both systems, and their list of kata often differ. Here is a list of the most common Okinawan forms, not necessarily in order.

Fukyugata 1-2 (Introductory)
Pinan 1-5 (Peaceful mind)
Naihanchi 1-3 (Hold your ground, also called Horse riding)
Seisan (Thirteen)
Wanshu (Chinese military envoy)
Ananku (Peace from the south)
Passai 1-2 (Breaking into the fortress)
Kusanku 1-2 (Chinese martial expert)
Gojushiho (Fifty-four steps)
Chinto (Chinese soldier)
Seiunchin (Walk far to conquer)
Sanchin (Three battles)
Chinte (Mysterious hand)
Shisochin (Fighting in four directions)
Tensho (Changing hands)
Rohai (Vision of a crane)

Jitte (Ten hands)
Wankan (King's crown)
Unsu (Hand in a cloud)

Japanese

There are so many different styles of Japanese karate that any list of kata is naturally going to leave out some patterns, so don't get your nose out of joint because I have left out your favorite form. Just glory in the fact that your kata is more exclusive than you thought.

Gichin Funakoshi, the "Father of Modern Karate," selected from the Okinawan kata he knew and adapted twenty-six of them into his new Shotokan school in the 1920s.

Heian 1-5 (Peaceful mind)
Tekki 1-3 (Iron horse)
Bassai 1-2 (Breaking into a fortress)
Kanku 1-2 (Look at the sky)
Gojushiho 1-2 (Fifty-four steps)
Chinte (Mysterious hand)
Sochin (Tranquil force)
Jion (A Buddhist temple)
Empi (Flight of the swallow)
Gankaku (Crane on a rock)
Jitte (Ten hands)
Hangetsu (Half moon)
Niji Shiho (Twenty-four steps)
Unsu (Hands in a cloud)
Wankan (King's crown)
Meikyo (Bright mirror)
Jiin (Love of truth)

A good website on Shotokan kata is www.shotokan-arts.com.

Korean

Post–World War II Korean arts such as Tang Soo Do borrowed from the Japanese and Okinawan karate styles. These are the ones that Jhoon Rhee taught when he was the first Korean to teach martial arts in America. Here are some of the patterns you might use if you practice one of those older Korean styles.

Pyungdan (Heian/Peaceful mind)

Chulgi (Tekki/Iron horse)

Bassai (Bassai/Breaking into the fortress)

Sipsoo (Jitte/Ten hands)

Soon after the origination of tae kwon do as a separate art in 1955, the masters, primarily General Choi, sought to develop a new, uniquely Korean, set of forms. However, the Chang-Hon (blue cottage) forms that he and Nam Tae Hi designed, with their low stances and powerful strikes, were very close to Shotokan karate kata. I have included the modern list of forms below. It is in a slightly different order than in the old original book by General Choi, *Taekwon-Do: The Art of Self-Defense*.

Chon-Ji (Heaven and earth)

Tan-Gun (The legendary founder of Korea)

Toe-San (Pseudonym of the patriot Ah Chang-Ho)

Won-Hyo (Monk who introduced Buddhism to the Silla Dynasty)

Yul-Gok (Pseudonym of philosopher Yi I)

Joong-Gun (Patriot Ahn Joong-Gun who assassinated a Japanese
   governor)

Toi-Gye (Pen name of the scholar Yi Hwang)

Hwa-Rang (The Hwa-Rang youth group of the Silla Dynasty)

Choong-Moo (Admiral who invented the first armored battleship)

Kwang-Gae (A king of the Koguryo Dynasty)

Po-Eun (Pseudonym of the poet Chong Mong-Chu)

Ge-Baek (A general of the Baek Je Dynasty)

Eui-Am (Pseudonym of Son Byong Hi, leader of the independence movement)

Choong-Jang (Pseudonym of General Kim Duk Ryang)

Juche (Philosophical idea that man is the master of his own fate)
    This pattern replaced the form Ko-Dang from the earlier lists.

Sam Il (Indicates the date of the independence movement—March 1, 1919)

Yoo-Sin (A general in the Silla Dynasty)

Choi Yong (A general in the Koryo Dynasty)

Yon Gae (A general in the Koguryo Dynasty)

Ul-ji (The general who defeated the Tang horde)

Moon-Moo (A king of the Silla Dynasty)

So-San (Pseudonym of the monk Choi Hyong Ung)

Se Jong (The king who devised the Korean alphabet)

Tong Il (Denotes the resolution to unify Korea)

A good website on tae kwon do forms is www.taekwondo-legacy.com.

After General Choi left the country, the new leaders of tae kwon do in Korea decided to design a completely different set of training patterns, one that would highlight the new emphasis on kicks. The World Tae Kwon Do Federation Palgwe forms are also known as "walking forms" because of their upright stances. Some schools prefer to use the Taegeuk forms for beginners, as they are more traditional.

Palgwe 1-8 (Represents the eight trigrams of the *I Ching*)

Taegeuk 1-8 (Universal origins [similar to above])

Koryo (The Korean dynasty from 918 to 1392)

Keumgang (Too strong to be broken, also Diamond)

TaeBaek (Bright light, also the old name of Mt. Baek Doo)

Pyongwon (Great plain)

Sipjin (Ten [decimal])

Jitae (Earth)

Cheonkwon (Sky)

Hansoo (Water)

Ilyo (Oneness)

Some other tae kwon do groups, such as the American Tae Kwon Do Association (the Song Am patterns), as well as individuals such as Jhoon Rhee, have also created their own patterns. This adds to the confusion of the typical tae kwon do student as he or she tries to figure out the history of the style's forms.

Profile: JOHN CHUNG

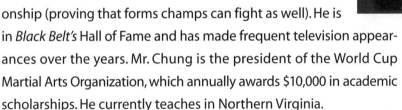

John Chung has been called the "king of kata." He was first rated number one in forms competition in 1981 and held that title for several years (he was named Forms Competitor of the Year in *Black Belt* magazine in 1981 and in *Inside Karate* in 1984). Besides being a world champion forms competitor, he simultaneously won a world fighting championship (proving that forms champs can fight as well). He is in *Black Belt's* Hall of Fame and has made frequent television appearances over the years. Mr. Chung is the president of the World Cup Martial Arts Organization, which annually awards $10,000 in academic scholarships. He currently teaches in Northern Virginia.

See www.johnchung.com.

Individual Forms

OK, here is the tough part. I don't have the space to picture all of the dozens of forms listed on the previous pages. Many excellent books will do that for you. Because this is a book on American systems, I am going to list a few of the more common patterns you'll probably use in your Americanized school. So let's start with the three I use at the beginning of my own Nam Seo Kwan curriculum. They are also used in a lot of

Figure 5-5 to Figure 5-27 Chon-Ji. Heaven and earth.

American tae kwon do schools around the country. Then I'm going to include a couple of karate forms, the first of the Heian series and the first of the Tekki series. You'll see these in many schools of karate.

Figure 5-28 to 5-53 Tan-Gun. Named for the
legendary founder of Korea in 2334 B.C.

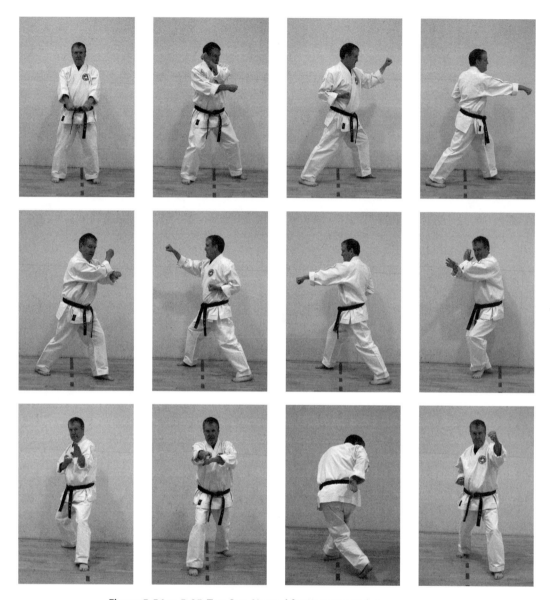

Figure 5-54 to 5-85 Toe-San. Named for Korean patriot and educator Ahn Ch'ang Ho, who was martyred in 1938.

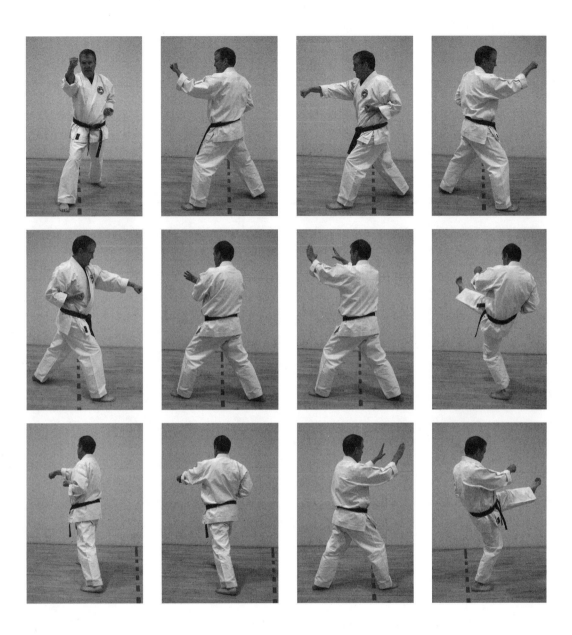

Figure 5-86 to 5-117 Heian 1. Heian means "peaceful," and these patterns are the first ones learned in many karate systems.

Figure 5-118 to 5-155 Tekki 1. Tekki means "iron horse" and is the
Japanese version of the older Naihanchi kata.

Questions from Chapter Five

■ Who said forms aren't very useful?

■ What is the literal meaning of "kata"?

■ What does *bunkai* mean?

■ What are the three stages of kata practice?

1. Learn the _____.

2. Work on _____.

3. Perform without _____.

■ Name two Japanese forms.

■ Name two Korean forms.

SIX

Sparring

History

For many young karate and tae kwon do students, sparring *is* the art. They join a dojo or dojang to compete in tournaments (to which they travel practically every weekend), and they proudly display their trophies at home next to their awards for soccer and baseball.

But to traditional martial artists, free-sparring is only a tiny part of their art. Did you know that sparring was only invented less than a hundred years ago? Karate was brought from Okinawa to Japan in the 1920s. In old Okinawa, the thought of practicing their self-defense art for the amusement of others or to gain trophies was unthinkable. But Japanese practitioners were used to engaging in kendo and judo contests and soon applied that attitude to the new import of karate-do.

The first public demonstration of *jiyu kumite* or "free-sparring" came in the fall of 1936 in Tokyo. As Japanese college karate clubs began to hold inter-school matches, the Okinawan teachers were horrified. How could karate techniques be practiced "free-style" without major injuries?

Even the famed Masatoshi Nakayama, who would go on to devise the first rules of competition, voiced his concerns about these contests: "Their original purpose was to promote friendship between clubs. . . . But the young blood of the students ran too hot to be satisfied with such tameness. . . . I feared karate would degenerate into a barbarous and dangerous technique."[1]

That was just before the beginning of World War II, which put a damper on the further development of karate as a sport. Nakayama, who spent the entire war working in China, soon came back to Japan to try to help establish karate once again. He developed rules for safe competition that were first used at the All Japan Grand Karate Tournament in October 1957.

But even then he had his doubts about free-sparring. He wrote, "As karate matches become popular, karate practitioners become too absorbed in winning. . . . Moreover, I cannot say whether the idea of free-fighting styles matches the soul of karate as taught by Master Funakoshi Gichin." Funakoshi had said that karate was to be practiced by "virtuous men" for a "higher purpose."

Sparring in America

If competitive sparring was controversial in Okinawa and Japan, it was a no-brainer in America. Westerners were used to and loved sports and competition. In fact, it was the sport of karate that put the martial arts on the map, so to speak. The "blood 'n' guts" era of the sport (see chapter one) proved that karate practitioners were just as tough as Western boxers or football players. They fought to win, and they didn't stop if they got hurt.

That image helped establish the martial arts in the United States as effective methods of fighting. The rules evolved, thankfully, in the ensuing decades, and today karate and tae kwon do tournaments are safe and fun events for kids of all ages.

Skipper Mullins vs. Fred Wren in the 1960s. In the early days of sparring, competitors did not wear today's protective padding. Naturally, injuries were common. Most schools today require hand and foot gear as well as helmets. Mouthpieces are cheap insurance for your pearly whites, and a cup is definitely mandatory for guys.

Sparring is a part of the training of practically everyone learning karate in this country, and most instructors encourage their students to participate in competitions of some kind, whether they are "open" (kind of a free-for-all) or "closed" (a single school or organization).

Sparring has many important benefits for students, including increased self-confidence, improvement of technique, and even development of the knowledge that they actually *can* withstand a kick to the stomach!

But while sport-type sparring is a popular and even useful training method, the martial artist would be wise to put it in its proper place. Self-defense situations don't have rules and don't generally occur at "sparring-distance." They are often up close and personal. I have known more than one tournament champion who got his clock cleaned in a real-life street fight because he didn't understand that concept.

American vs. Olympic-Style Tae Kwon Do

Back in chapter one I spoke briefly about the development of the Kukki-won tae kwon do style and how it was accepted as an Olympic sport in 2000 with different rules than had been traditionally used by tae kwon do fighters. There is often a big divide between Olympic competition and the American open tournament scene ("open" because they are open to anyone who wants to enter). The two sides often don't even acknowledge one another. Olympic stylists dismiss the open stylists as not being in the "modern" sport world, and the open tournament competitors say the Olympic fighters are too restricted and unrealistic in their techniques.

Both approaches have advantages and disadvantages. In fact, we have several schools in the A-KaTo that train for both kinds of competition. But probably the most telling comment I've heard is from a young black belt who has won trophies and medals in both. He told me he liked competing in the Olympic style better (he is a great kicker). When I asked why, he said he didn't like getting punched in the face in those American-style open tournaments! As you'll remember from our discussion in chapter one, Olympic tae kwon do doesn't allow head punches at all.

Since I practice and teach American tae kwon do, we are going to concentrate on those techniques and principles in this chapter.

One-Step Sparring Drills

Beginners usually approach the whole idea of sparring with some trepidation. That's why in most schools students are taught the basics of distance and targeting with a two-person drill called "one-step sparring."

One student is assigned the role of attacker and the other one assumes the defender role. The attacker steps in with a single punching attack, and the defender proceeds to execute a simple defense and counterattack. This way, control is maintained, and no one gets hurt as the students practice their defensive and offensive combinations for eventual use in a more random practice.

In my own Nam Seo Kwan style, I have devised six prearranged one-steps that students must learn to advance to their next belt rank (this goes up to green belt with a blue stripe). At that rank I allow students to make up their own combinations as they progress in the system. Some schools have many more predetermined sets (kenpo karate, for example, has hundreds—with cool names like "thundering hammers" and "intercepting the ram").

Because the possibilities are truly endless, I can only show you a few drills on these pages. The following is Nam Seo Kwan's set of six. By the way, if you want to learn more one-steps, in 2006 I shot an instructional

DVD that contains "One Hundred and One One-Steps." Go to our website at www.akato.org.

One

Figure 6-2. After bowing, the two partners face each other in the ready position. As the defender, yell to signal that you are ready for the attack.

Figure 6-3. The attacker steps back with a yell and a low block.

Figure 6-4. As the attacker steps forward with a punch to the face, shift into a back stance and execute an inside block.

Figure 6-5. Keep your front hand moving and immediately strike with a backfist.

Figure 6-6. Finish the counterattack with a reverse punch to the solar plexus. You should yell on the finishing technique.

Figure 6-7. Now step back into a guarding stance.

Figure 6-2

Figure 6-3

Figure 6-4

Figure 6-5

Figure 6-6

Figure 6-7

Figure 6-8

Figure 6-9

Figure 6-10

Two

Figure 6-8. This sequence starts with a knife-hand block executed in a back stance.

Figure 6-9. Reverse punch to the solar plexus.

Figure 6-10. Finish with a palm heel strike to the face.

Figure 6-11

Three

Figure 6-11. Step back and out of the way of the punch and execute an outside block.

Figure 6-12. Front kick to groin level.

Figure 6-13. Set the kicking foot down into a horse stance as you punch to the solar plexus.

Figure 6-14. A second punch quickly follows.

Figure 6-12

Figure 6-13

Figure 6-14

Figure 6-15

Figure 6-16

Figure 6-17

Four

Figure 6-15. Step to the side to avoid the incoming punch. At the same time, do an outside block.

Figure 6-16. Do a front leg roundhouse kick to the attacker's chest.

Figure 6-17. Set your foot down, and finish with a reverse punch.

Five

Figure 6-18. Step to the side (off-line), and inside block with an open hand. Note the other hand placed under the elbow.

Figure 6-19. Pull the attacker into a chop to his mid-section.

Figure 6-20. The same hand circles up and strikes in the back of his neck.

Figure 6-21. Finish by driving your knee into his ribs.

Figure 6-18

Figure 6-19

Figure 6-20

Figure 6-21

Six

Figure 6-22. Step just outside of the attacker's front foot as he steps in to punch. Execute an outside block, and at the same time strike with an open palm to his throat. It is important that you step, block, and strike simultaneously.

Figure 6-23. The striking hand quickly circles into a chop to the attacker's collarbone.

Figure 6-24. Grab his collar for leverage as you swing your back leg up and behind his front leg.

Figure 6-25. This is one of the basic sweeps taught in judo training. The back of your calf muscle sweeps into the back of the attacker's calf muscle. At the same time, push his upper body back.

Figure 6-26. You can finish the sequence with a stomp to his downed body.

Figure 6-22

Figure 6-23

Figure 6-24

Figure 6-25

Figure 6-26

Free-Style Sparring

After you have learned something about distancing and targeting with your one-step sparring drills, you can progress into a more unpredictable, yet controlled, fighting practice with another student. This is called "free-style" sparring.

Most beginners want to know some techniques. "What should I do?" is a common question. I'll get into that in a couple pages, but first I want to give you a list of some tips for better sparring.

1. *Relax.* Everyone tenses up when they begin sparring. That is natural, but you are slower when you're tense, and you tire more quickly. I realize that it's easier said than done, but with practice and experience it will become easier to loosen up.

2. *Think.* A lot of people "blank out" when they spar. While at the more advanced stages that can actually be good (remember the concept of "no mind"?) at the beginning levels, you want to be able to analyze an opponent's moves and come up with your own counter moves on the spot.

3. *Don't change your own style.* Don't change your own preferences according to the other person's style of fighting. If you like to spar with your left side out, for example, don't allow the opponent to force you to change to your weaker side. In other words, fight *your* fight, not his.

4. *Move your feet.* Don't just stand there like a statue. You want to be light on your feet. Move from side to side, forward and back. But don't just run backward at full speed—you'll run out of room. While evasiveness is good, you'll eventually have to be aggressive and move in to score your points.

5. *Move your body.* Yes, I know if you move your feet, your body moves also. But here I am talking about "bobbing and weaving" such as a boxer does. You can evade a blow by leaning or ducking out of the

way to avoid taking the full force of the punch or kick. You can also "feint" with your head. In other words, make a quick movement to test the opponent's reaction. You can even fake with your body, making it appear as though you are about to hit to one area but then striking out to another target.

6. *Show confidence.* A lot of sparring is mental. If you show your opponent that you are not afraid, it makes her more cautious and not as likely to just storm in on you. In most sports, this is known as "psyching out" your opponent. You do this with your expression (especially your eyes) and your body language. Even if you don't have confidence, try to show some, and it will help build up those feelings inside of you.

7. *Use combinations.* Variety is not only the spice of life but also the best way to score on an opponent. If she doesn't know what to expect, it becomes harder for her to block and counter your techniques. If you become predictable, you will become a sitting duck—and what's more predictable than a duck just sitting there?

8. *Be in shape.* Needless to say you have to be able to last the duration of the match (or maybe several in a row in an advanced class or on a promotional exam). And if you are more physically fit than your opponent, you can easily tire him out. While you can't condition your joints, groin, or nose to take a blow, you can work on strengthening the muscles around your midsection to protect your organs.

9. *Obey the rules.* This should go without saying in a classroom situation or even in a tournament. The martial arts should teach you respect for others. We'll cover some of the rules of competition in a few pages.

10. *Work on your speed and timing.* Timing is the knowledge of when to hit an opponent. Speed is your ability to do it in the minimum amount of time. All the great champions have these qualities. In fact, world champion Benny "the Jet" Urquidez says speed is the

most important physical element for competition.[2] He also says it is easier to develop punching speed than kicking speed simply because your legs are heavier and further away from your opponent's targets.

11. *Hit the right spots.* Raymond McCallum, one of the great champions of the 1970s, used to preach "technique to target." What he meant was you must do more than just punch or kick *toward* your opponent. You have to actually hit the approved target areas to score. He visualized his fist or his foot hitting the solar plexus, the back of the head, etc. You can practice this during sparring class and you can train on a heavy bag, repeatedly hitting the same exact smudge on the bag with your round kick or ridgehand.

12. *Practice with bag work.* Hitting the bag also can be a great way to work on power and on your ability to deliver a powerful strike with the proper body mechanics. Even if you are not training for full-contact competition, I think bag work is an essential part of becoming a better fighter.

13. *Control and place your techniques.* The only problem with hitting the heavy bag is that you train to penetrate the surface and deliver a punishing impact (good in self-defense or full-contact, not so good in point-competition). Many instructors talk about controlling your strikes or "pulling your punches." I don't like to use that term because I don't want to "pull back" on the extension of my punch or kick. Instead, I want to concentrate on "placing" my technique in an exact spot. This means not only on the precise target area but just touching the surface of that area. So after you smash the heavy bag for a while, go back and practice using control—that is, just "kissing" the surface of the bag with your kicks or punches. A good fighter has enough body control to just nick your uniform, knock the wind out of you, or break your ribs.

14. *Get to know your opponent.* This is tough to do in a minute or two,

but if you are able to recognize an opponent's tendencies and strengths and weaknesses, you will have a much better chance of winning the contest. How do you do that? You test or feint. All fighters have habits. The really good ones know how to disguise them, but you are probably not going to be facing that kind of opponent unless you are in the black belt divisions. So, for example, take a couple of jabs at her face. If she moves back more than once, you'll know it is probably a habit, and that will open up an opportunity for you to kick her when she moves back.

Figure 6-27

Figure 6-28

Figure 6-27. If you ever run up against opponents with a little boxing training, you can count on the fact that they've gotten their bell rung a few times and realized they could keep on fighting. I dare say many karate and tae kwon do students (at least those below brown or red belt) have probably never been smashed in the face or jaw unless their school is into full-contact sparring. While full-contact sparring or boxing is not for everyone, I do want my students to know they can take some contact and still keep fighting. That's why we use padded gloves and boots for sparring—that, and the fact that it protects fingers and toes.

Figure 6-28. You can often measure up your opponent based on body type. The guy on the left is probably slower but more powerful. The fighter on the right is likely faster but not as strong. However, you might do well to remember Sir Isaac Newton's second law of physics—basically, velocity times mass equals impact. That means the faster someone is, the harder they hit (even the little guys).

Figure 6-29. Even though most schools don't allow students to make contact until more advanced stages, you might want to develop the

Figure 6-29   **Figure 6-30**   **Figure 6-31**

toughness to take a blow. "Slapping-drills" are used by experienced fighters to steel themselves mentally to the sting of a kick or punch. Another option is "body-work," in which you and a sparring partner practice intentionally hitting each other in the gut with boxing gloves.

Figure 6-30. In full-contact sparring (not for beginners), the kicks often don't snap back. The idea is not to control depth or impact but to just slam the foot into the opponent's body as hard as you can. Thai boxers, for example, use their famous whipping kicks to break down an opponent's resistance. This photo shows a couple of kickboxers from the World Combat League.

Figure 6-32

Figure 6-31. A straight punch is faster than a roundhouse swing because of the shorter distance traveled. It also tends to have more of a "breaking" impact, although this is probably more important in self-defense situations. In point competition, however, a swinging technique, like this ridgehand to the side of your opponent's helmet, is harder to block and thus easier to score with.

Figure 6-32. If an opponent has fast hands, use your kicks to distract him and slow him down. If he has good kicks, however, get in close to jam him and smother those legs.

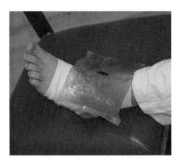

Figure 6-33

Figure 6-33. If you sustain a minor injury in sparring (the most common kind) you should use RICE. I don't mean Chinese take-out; I mean the well-known acronym for Rest, Ice, Compression, and Elevation.

Don't try to fight through the pain. Stop the match and take a break. Put some ice (crushed in a cloth wrap) on the bruise to prevent swelling and elevate it to keep blood from collecting at the site. Wrapping the injury also keeps the swelling in check.

Of course, if the situation demands, see a doctor.

You will be relieved to know that trips to the emergency room are extremely rare. Still, karate and tae kwon do are semi-contact activities, and accidents will happen.

Tournament Competition

There are now so many different American sport karate organizations, each with a different set of rules, that I cannot give you a list of practices or rules that is going to apply everywhere, so always check before you step into the ring. Still, here are some general guidelines.

You'll find a karate tournament held somewhere almost every weekend (in America almost all open events are called "karate" championships). They'll be in places ranging from YMCA gyms to hotel ballrooms. They often have grandiose sounding names like the "World Games" or the "Nationals" in spite of the fact that the competitors only come from a twenty-mile radius. The truth is, there are very few truly national events, so be skeptical of someone who claims to be the "U.S. Champion." He probably won it in an elementary school gym in Peoria.

The sparring area (the ring) will be about twenty feet square. There are an odd number of judges, usually a center referee and two corner judges. That way, the majority rules in awarding a point.

Points are given if a technique strikes an approved target area with enough focus and balance to have caused damage if it had penetrated a little bit further. If you hit too hard, however, you can be penalized for excessive contact. In some organizations, hitting in the face, however lightly, is considered excessive (usually this applies in the children's divisions). Sport targets do not include the eyes, throat, and knees because they are too easily injured.

In the early days of American tournaments, when I was competing, every score was just one point. Soon the powers that be decided that because it was harder to hit a target with a foot than with a hand, the fighter should get two points for a kick. That is the rule today in most competitions, although in some parts of the country a groin kick is still worth only one point (in some tournaments groin kicks are outlawed altogether). And in some organizations a really difficult kick, like a jumping side kick, earns you three points. See what I mean about checking the rules in your area!

Incidentally, back in those dark ages when I was fighting in tournaments, they didn't have enough kids to divide up into separate rank divisions, so all the kids, from twelve-year-old white belts to fifteen-year-old brown belts went into the same division. And there usually weren't enough women to split up either, so it was common to see women white belts sparring women brown belts.

Today there can be dozens of divisions for both sparring and kata. They are split up by rank and by age. Adult divisions also usually have weight classes. In some small events you might have to win just one or two matches for a trophy, but in the large tournaments you might have to win ten or more matches.

Penalties include running out of the ring, hitting toward an illegal target area, and, in children's divisions, hitting in the face. Yelling at a referee would be considered a penalty (karate is, after all, different than purely American sports like baseball).

I have already mentioned that Olympic tae kwon do is a completely different animal than American open tournaments. If you are going to compete in an Olympic-style event, make sure you understand those rules.

The last thing I want to say about tournaments is they can teach valuable lessons for life or they can reinforce all the bad things that you hear about sporting competitions. Winning feels good, but losing feels bad. Unfortunately, most people are not going to win a trophy or medal in a tournament. Your goal should be to do your best and to learn something positive from the competition (maybe it's just to keep your hands up next time). Frankly, I think kids should learn how to overcome defeat because life will be easier to handle as they face difficult situations later on. If you learn how to not make excuses, you will be stronger and ultimately more successful.

There are many good books on sparring techniques (see the bibliography), so I am only going to include a few of my own favorites to get you started. Pay attention to the principles that these sequences teach.

Sparring Techniques

Figure 6-34 to 6-35. The "C-shaped" punch, low and then high, can be

an easy way to score. This is the old "misdirection" principle that you'll see in other sports like tennis. Hit toward one spot, and then when your opponent reacts, go to the opposite side of the court.

Figure 6-34   Figure 6-35

Figure 6-36

Figure 6-37

Figure 6-38

Figure 6-36 to 6-38. The same principle applies to a kick. Roundkick low to the groin, and when your opponent reaches down to block, snap your foot up to his face.

Figure 6-39 to 6-41. Here's a combination from boxing. Shoot out a right jab. Follow it up with a left hook punch. This gets the opponent thinking about protecting himself from your attacks coming in from the left and right. Then uppercut right up between his gloves. Again, the principle is "misdirection." Hit from high, from low, from left, and from right.

Figure 6-39

Figure 6-40

Figure 6-41

Figure 6-42   Figure 6-43

Figure 6-42 to 6-43. Shoot out a jab to his face and at the same time slide your back foot forward. The jab distracts him and blocks his vision, preventing him from seeing how you just stepped much closer. Now you are in position for a side thrust kick to his ribs. Note that I grab his front sleeve to prevent him from dropping his elbow to try to block the kick.

Figure 6-44 to 6-46. World champion Skipper Mullins taught me this one. From an open stance (both facing the same direction), bring your back leg up and point the knee toward his chest. He will react to your motion as if you were going to kick him in the body, that is, his attention is focused on your leg. That's when you shoot out a punch to

Figure 6-44   Figure 6-45   Figure 6-46

his head. Note that I am pushing his hands down to prevent him from blocking.

Questions from Chapter Six

■ Sparring has been done for centuries. True or false?

■ One-step sparring drills are a good introduction to the principles of fighting. True or false?

■ Sparring techniques always work great in a real street fight. True or false?

■ Open karate tournaments and Olympic tae kwon do competition have the same rules. True or false?

■ Name a target area that is illegal in a tournament match.

SEVEN

Self-Defense

The news media gave us endless coverage of the tragedy of thirty-three people murdered on the Virginia Tech campus in 2007. But they didn't cover the other thirty to forty murders that occurred in America on the very same day. Why? Because that much violence in one place is "news," but violence spread out across the nation—well, that's just everyday life in the United States.

You have a greater chance of becoming a victim of violent crime than you do of being injured in an auto accident. Now, if you fasten your seat belt every time you get in your car and if you stop at a red light instead of trying to speed through it, then why, in heaven's name, aren't you taking the same kind of precautions about your personal safety when it comes to crime?

PRE-fight

Before I get into specific techniques that karate and tae kwon do can teach you, I want to cover some of what I like to call the PRE-fight check. In other words, before you are forced to fight, before you have to use some of your martial arts moves, I want you to be in the habit of practicing these few simple rules.

The acronym "P-R-E" stands for prevention, recognition, and escape. You can go a long ways toward avoiding a confrontation with a criminal if you first practice these and make them a part of your daily routine.

A long time ago, I saw a television show in which former Chicago detective J. J. Bittenbinder illustrated the principle of not being an easy target with a joke. I'll paraphrase it here because it's funny and it helps me—and hopefully you—to remember the concept.

Two guys are sleeping in a tent on a camping trip. They wake up to hear a hungry bear clawing his way in. One guy grabs his running shoes to put them on. The other guy says, "What are you doing? You can't outrun a bear!"

He replies, "I don't have to outrun the bear. I just have to outrun you!"

Here's the point. The predator, the criminal in our case, is going to go for the closest victim, the easiest prey. A lion stalking a herd of antelope is not going to chase after the biggest one with the huge horns. He doesn't want a fight—he wants dinner. He is going to go for the straggler, the one not looking for danger. Don't be the little antelope.

Prevention

I was a Boy Scout, and I still remember the motto, "Be Prepared." Boy Scouts take precautions like having insect repellent and drinking water in their backpacks. What kind of precautions do you take in your everyday life?

I know you have heard the typical crime prevention tips: lock your house when you leave, don't open the door to strangers, don't leave your keys in the ignition, don't put your name and phone number on that Internet chat site, etc. But your life is so busy. You don't have time to buy that extra deadbolt for the house. You are preoccupied with the job and the kids, and you can't pay attention to every little thing. Besides, what are the chances something will happen to you?

Unfortunately that's what millions of crime victims every year thought, too!

There are plenty of good books on self-defense that go into a lot more detail than I am going to give you here, but this is a list of a few practical prevention tips.

Lock your doors and windows. Fifty percent of home break-ins are through unlocked doors and windows. So if you lock your house, you can decrease your chance of burglary.

Get to know your neighbors or, better yet, start a neighborhood watch group.

Keep at least a quarter of a tank of gas in your car, so you don't have to stop at a gas station in a bad part of town or late at night.

Check the backseat of your car before you get in.

Don't leave your keys in the car when you leave.

Keep your car locked at all times, even when driving.

Park under a street lamp if you know you'll be leaving the office or the shopping mall after dark.

Ask a security guard at the mall to walk you to your car if it's late (don't be embarrassed—that's what they're there for).

Hold your purse or your expensive camera up under your arm and not dangling by a strap.

Take a friend with you to the mall (especially important for kids and teenagers).

Try not to use public restrooms alone.

If you absolutely have to use an outside ATM, scan the area first. Better yet, make sure you don't have to use it at all. Plan ahead.

Don't jog or walk with earphones from your music player blotting out all external sound.

If someone says he is a police officer and is not wearing a uniform, request a uniformed backup.

Stay away from people who abuse alcohol and drugs. Some estimate that about 75 percent of sexual assault cases involve an attacker who had been drinking. Now, I don't presume to tell you that you shouldn't drink at all. But you should be aware that both alcohol and drugs lower inhibitions and make a person's behavior unpredictable—yours included. They also act as pain suppressants, so your self-defense techniques have less of an effect on someone who is drunk or high.

Don't give your full name, phone number, or address to someone you don't know on the Internet. If a stranger on the street came up and asked for your name and phone number, would you give it to him?

Speaking of strangers, tell your kids not to talk to them, and then practice the same thing yourself. A common practice of muggers is to come up and ask someone for directions or for the time. I know you don't want to seem rude, but just say, "No"—or at least keep your antennae up.

Recognition

You have to be able to recognize danger, not be oblivious to it—this is called awareness. I know Gichin Funakoshi said there is "no first strike" in karate, but I'll bet he would agree that we should be constantly aware. What I mean here is that our "first strike" is one of tactical awareness and of the ability to defend ourselves aggressively and without hesitation. This is a shocking surprise to most felons.

Let's say you have obeyed most of the above rules of prevention. Congratulations, you have certainly reduced your potential for becoming a victim of crime. But let's face it—sometimes people end up in the wrong place at the wrong time. Is your level of recognition, your awareness, at the stage where you are able to see something bad coming?

Going back to that terrible shooting at Virginia Tech, there seemed to have been signs that the young man was disturbed. In retrospect people remembered things that suggested he might do something heinous. But most of his acquaintances brushed it off as just "weirdness."

This is a common scenario. The rape victim says the guy had been getting more aggressive during the past couple of dates. The carjack victim says he noticed that red pickup following him, but he didn't think anything of it. Recognition abilities mean perceiving a situation or person as dangerous. Recognition means noticing his body language, the way he is standing, his facial expression, and his tone of voice.

Awareness often means just trusting your instincts. If you feel uneasy in a situation, there is probably good reason for your uneasiness. Keep your eyes open at all times. Some people have poor instincts because don't believe anything bad could happen to them. A common problem with kids and teenagers is that peer pressure encourages them to act "cool" and nonchalant. That's the opposite of the kind of attitude you should have. Practice keeping your eyes and ears open and alert.

Gavin de Becker, in his excellent book *The Gift of Fear*, not only presents some sobering statistics on violence in America but says he does so to convince people of the very real likelihood that they or someone they love will be a victim. He says such a belief is a key element in recognizing the presence of danger.[1]

He makes the interesting point that of all the animals on the planet, we humans are the only ones who rationalize away our natural instincts. "No animal in the wild," he writes, "suddenly overcome with fear, would spend any of its mental energy thinking, 'It's probably nothing!'" A rabbit smells a wolf and runs. A human senses something not quite right and says, "Oh, I'm just being paranoid." De Becker says we must trust our natural instincts and recognize danger when it's there.

Karate master Randall Hassell, in *Karate: Zen, Pen, and Sword*, points out that "awareness is not a quantitative 'thing' that can be learned; it is a state of mind that must be realized."[2] What is your normal state of awareness?

The Department of Homeland Security has an advisory system that uses colored alert levels. If you can adapt that system to your everyday life, maybe you can get a feel for your level of awareness.

According to the government, green is a *low* threat level. Should you ever be in this low state of awareness? Well, maybe in your own home with all the doors locked.

Next is blue, or *guarded*. Whenever you go outside—to pick up your newspaper, for example, or to get into your car—you should be in this stage. Even at work or school it would be a good idea to be on your guard.

Yellow is the *elevated* stage of alertness. Let's say you're in an unfamiliar setting, a parking garage or a busy street corner in a big city. Try to look like you know where you're going. Muggers scan for people who look out of place and unaware.

Orange alert is what Homeland Security calls a *high* risk stage. On your personal defense scale, I'd say this is the stage where your instincts are telling you something is not right. Like I said before, many people ignore their own uneasiness, thinking they are just being paranoid. Trust your feelings! For example, if a stranger offers to carry your bags and you feel uncomfortable, say in a firm voice: "No!" If he insists, don't be afraid to call out for help.

Red alert means *severe* risk of attack. (I can hear the computer voice on the U.S.S. Enterprise warning, "Red alert!") This is when someone kicks in your front door, your date has started ripping your blouse, or the creep demands your wallet. You still have a chance to survive, but it depends on your actions from here on out. What are you going to do now?

Alert Levels

Green—Low risk of attack

Blue—Guarded risk

Yellow—Elevated risk

Orange—High risk

Red—Severe risk

5,200,000 Violent crimes in the United States **2005**

52.3% perpetrated by strangers / 47.7% by someone the victim knew

So about half the time it's someone you know who's going to victimize you.

192,000 Rape/sexual assault

34.9% perpetrated by strangers / 65.1% by someone the victim knew

Over 65% of the time it's someone you know (remember, these are just the assaults reported to police).

625,000 Robberies

79.9% perpetrated by strangers / 20.1% by someone the victim knew

143,000 robberies with injury to victim

So about 27% of the victims are hurt in a robbery (but much more likely if the robber is a stranger).

And there are an additional 65,000 victims injured in an attempted robbery without property taken.

4,357,000 Assaults

49.1% perpetrated by strangers / 50.9% by someone the victim knew

That makes it about 50/50 that if you get into a fight it will be with a stranger.

Most of the time alcohol is involved.

1,126,000 Injuries requiring treatment from an assault

If you get into a fight, about a fourth of the time you'll end up in an emergency room.

407,000 Reported Purse snatching/pocket picking

2,320,000 Persons incarcerated in the United States at the end of 2005.

7,000,000 Persons on probation and parole

So there are over nine million criminals under correctional supervision in the United States.

To put that in perspective, there are only ten states with populations larger than nine million people.

Source: Department of Justice

Crime in America: these are the figures from the U.S. Department of Justice for 2005 (the latest stats at the time of this writing). Remember that a lot of crime in this country is not reported to the police. Just take these numbers as a low estimate of actual violent crimes.

When I was a kid, we used to play the "slug bug" game on those long auto trips. We'd look for Volkswagen Beetles and yell out "slug bug" if we were the first to see them. This kind of game is actually useful for developing your sense of awareness and recognition. Try it at a shopping mall. For example, look for women with handbags, or men with beards. These "awareness exercises" get you used to scanning your surroundings.

Now take this a step farther and pretend you're a mugger or purse-snatcher. Look for the easy victim, someone who is walking along unawares. It is surprising how many people allow themselves to be the slowest antelope in the herd.

Escape

As the old saying goes, "the best defense is a good offense." Well, maybe that works in a sports competition in which the person or team with the most points wins. But in a self-defense situation, the best defense, as one famous movie sensei said, is "no be there!" Backing off or even running away is preferable to having to hit or be hit in an actual physical confrontation.

I tell my young students to run if someone tries to grab them or hurt them, and kids seem to get the concept. However, adults (maybe I should say "guys") sometimes think running brands them as "chicken." But believe me, you'd rather be a live chicken than a dead duck.

Other people (both men and women) can go into shock and freeze, not being able to escape—or do much of anything except stand there in shock. The best way to avoid either freezing or trying to foolishly stand your ground is to decide ahead of time that you are going to make a break for it if the situation looks bad. Simply put, that means having a plan.

Now, your plan could be as simple as mentally rehearsing a scream for help and running. Or it could take more elaborate dimensions. Do you have a plan for escaping from your home if it were on fire? I'm sure you know where all the doors in your house are. Perhaps you have even planned ahead and have a collapsible ladder by the upstairs window.

Before a commercial airliner takes off, the flight attendants are required to point out the exits. Most people don't pay attention. I do. I also scan for the exits when I go into a restaurant or store. I always want to have a plan.

In a confrontation, your reaction will probably be based on not wanting to get hurt rather than on survival, but I am telling you that it can't be. You might have to jump out of your car when a carjacker jumps in. Yes, you might get hurt, but you will survive. Start planning like a survivor right now. Plan to escape however you can.

Police statistics show that if you allow yourself to be taken to a secondary crime scene, your chances of survival go way down. Do not get into a vehicle even if someone promises not to hurt you. I remember a scene in *Pirates of the Caribbean* in which Will Turner protests that the pirate Jack Sparrow has cheated in a fight. Captain Jack simply replies, "Pirate!" The unsaid message was: *bad guys lie.* You should scream, fight, and run.

Physical and Psychological Techniques

We are about to get into some actual physical techniques that will help you be a survivor. We'll assume your escape has been cut off and you have to make a stand. Here is where all your karate and tae kwon do training is going to pay off, right?

Probably—well, maybe. I have heard too many stories of martial arts experts who have frozen in the face of a real life assailant. How could that be? A "deer caught in the headlights" just stands in the middle of the road waiting for the inevitable crash. You see, a deer's natural instinct is to remain perfectly still when it senses danger. This may work in the forest, when an approaching wolf cannot see or hear the deer, but a Mack truck is a different beast altogether. But the poor deer has no frame of reference for the truck; it has never had that kind of enemy.

Now the typical martial arts student has practiced his self-defense techniques many times in class. His partner assumes the "front choke" posture, and he does his escape and counterstrike, and he thinks he is ready for the real thing.

A real street encounter is nothing like having a compliant partner rest his hands on your neck waiting for you to do your technique. The real predator grabs your throat violently. He squeezes so hard your breath is caught short, and immediately your eyes bug out and your vision starts to go black! Maybe he is slamming your head into a concrete wall. Even though you have trained, perhaps for years, you have no frame of reference for this kind of savagery. You momentarily freeze. Unfortunately, a moment is all it takes for you to fall unconscious.

All the knowledge in the world won't help you if you are psychologically unable to instantaneously fight back and perhaps even hurt someone. The great Japanese swordsman Musashi wrote, "The combat is decided before the swords are first crossed." You have to be able to react under stress, and you have to have already made the mental decision to use force if your safety or that of your loved ones is threatened.

Adrenal Fighting

Adrenaline release is another name for the "fight or flight" response. Ideally, as we've said, you want to be able to harness or at least control this burst of chemicals your system releases under intense stress. But how do you do that? The only way is to train in such a way that you actually produce an adrenal effect.

One of our female black belts conducts women's self-defense classes all over the state. At the culmination of several sessions, she has the students face a padded attacker. The assailant doesn't just reach out and grab them to see if they can hit him hard—he curses at them, he yells out what he's going to do to them, he pulls their hair and throws them to the ground. I've seen even trained black belts wilt under that kind of pressure. Under adrenal stress, all those karate techniques don't seem to be nearly as effective. The problem is that the mind cannot think straight, and so the body doesn't respond with those perfect kicks and punches.

It is my opinion that typical karate and tae kwon do training in the United States focuses on developing a few precise techniques. But real fights do not consist of perfect roundhouse kicks and reverse punches. They are ugly and sloppy, and you had better be prepared. Payton Quinn, in his excellent book *Real Fighting,* says the principles of combat are more important than the actual techniques.[3] He says the effectiveness of any technique you might attempt to use will vary depending on the size of the attacker, the speed and angle of the attack, the physical settings, and so forth. So any predetermined single or even series of self-defense techniques can only serve to give you concepts rather than actual specifics you could use to defend yourself in an actual encounter.

Remember the scientist in *Jurassic Park* talking about chaos theory? Everything is random, and that leads to unpredictable results. So learning the techniques on the following pages is the easy part—delivering them under pressure is the hard part.

In another of my favorite self-defense books, *Attack Proof: The Ultimate Guide to Personal Protection,* the authors say that a real life-or-death street fight does not even remotely resemble a kata, one-steps, or a sparring match.[4] Their approach is called "guided chaos" and is based on the idea that a real fight is, well, chaotic. That means you cannot rely

The interview

Don't lose your cool, but channel your anger.

on the situation to be predictable. Your opponent may punch you, slap you, spit on you, tackle you, or just shoot you from six feet away. How in the world are you going to know what to do in every situation?

As I write this, there was a funeral held last week for a Dallas police officer who was shot and killed by a murder suspect as he attempted to get him out of a car. Police officers spend weeks, months, and years training in realistic scenarios, and yet they often put themselves at unnecessary risk in high-adrenaline situations. If highly trained cops and soldiers are wounded and killed on a regular basis, what hope does a weekend warrior green belt have in that real-life encounter with a desperate street thug or a drunken road rager? Well, the good news is there are many things you can do to increase your chances of survival. Go back and reread that section on PRE-fight. The best self-defense is not having to use physical techniques.

Unless a mugger or rapist just rushes up and tackles you, there will usually be what criminologists call "the interview." The attacker is sizing you up. The predator asks for a cigarette, for directions, anything to distract you and put you off guard. The good manners instilled in us as children can sometimes delay our response. If you feel uneasy, even in the slightest, firmly respond, "Sorry, no!" and back away.

Another "interview" technique could be an accusation or insult—"You looking at me?" Unless you are in immediate danger of being harmed, be a pacifist. Apologize, back down, do whatever is necessary to de-escalate the situation. Fights are seldom worth the risks because you simply don't know with whom you are dealing. Self-defense isn't about saving face, it's about saving your health and possibly your life. A martial artist should have self-control—that means not losing your temper. An out-of-control temper is detrimental to your ability to defend yourself in a confrontation. When you lose your cool, you also lose your ability to think clearly and to be physically relaxed and ready to respond to an attack.

Excessive force and the law

But not losing your temper is not the same thing as channeling your anger. Self-defense expert Jeff Cooper asks, how do we cultivate an immediate and aggressive response to attack? He says it boils down to being angry that someone would prey on you. They are simply bad people, and you are justified in resenting their behavior. Cooper points out that anger and fear are two very close emotions. The key is to turn your fear into anger and allow yourself to get mad at the predator who is trying to hurt you or your loved ones.[5]

In most states, the law permits you to defend yourself with force equal to the level of the threat or attack against you. In other words, if a jerk calls you a name and even pushes you, it's illegal for you to kick him in the groin. If he punches you in the nose, and you pull out your pistol and shoot him in the chest, that will most likely be considered excessive force under the law. But you should also know that you are generally allowed to use even "deadly force" if the attack is committed with deadly force. That means if he pulls a knife on you, you are probably within your legal rights to use your gun. But this whole subject of when you can legally defend yourself is complicated and varies from state to state. You had better check out the laws wherever you live.

Should You Carry a Gun?

You should only carry a gun if you are licensed in your state. That means you have had the professional training required to obtain the permit. The training will cover things like having the mind-set to actually shoot someone (not unlike the response training we have talked about in empty-hand defense). Gun instructors also teach that it is very difficult to get your weapon out and ready to use if someone suddenly attacks you. It is also surprisingly easy to take a gun away from a frightened and untrained person.

Women and self-defense

By the way, self-defense *against* a gun- or knife-wielding opponent is beyond the scope of this little book, so look at the bibliography for my recommendations.

Women are just as likely to be victims of a robbery as men, and they are far more likely to be victims of sexual assault. Most women realize this fact, and that's why so many women are signing up for karate and tae kwon do lessons. Unfortunately, many instructors of said "self-defense arts" are not adequately equipped to deal with the intricacies of rape prevention. It is a complicated subject made even more so by the fact that many female students in a typical martial arts class have been victims themselves. According to the Rape Crisis Center, one in four women will be sexually assaulted in her lifetime. That is a frightening statistic to think about.

Another frightening statistic is that sexual assault is more likely to be perpetrated by someone the victim knows, i.e., boyfriend, ex-husband, relative, co-worker, neighbor. That means you must keep your guard up at all times. I know you don't want to think badly of someone you know, but if he gets too aggressive and won't respect your "no," then you must stand up for yourself immediately and firmly. Often this will work, but you must also be prepared to physically defend yourself.

Now I know some people say that if you attempt to fight back you run a greater risk of being injured. Statistically that is true (but only by a small percentage), but the stats also show that you have a greater chance of escaping from an assault by an acquaintance if you fight back. And it is also true that women who fought back experience fewer emotional scars. Still, only you can make the determination of whether to fight back, but you'll need to be prepared no matter what.

Women, here are some signs to look out for: Is he controlling or pushy? Does he tell jokes that are degrading to women? Does he drink to excess? All the principles of prevention, recognition, and escape apply here. There are plenty of good books on this topic (many of which are listed in the back of this book), and I suggest that if you are a female student, or an instructor, you need to become more knowledgeable in this area.

Ground Fighting

If you have flipped through your cable television channels, you've seen some Ultimate Fighting matches. These events (started by the Gracie JuJutsu family) have shown that stand-up, striking-style martial arts have some real disadvantages in a knock-down, drag-out brawl. Contrary to popular opinion, most fights do not "end up on the ground," but enough of them do that karate and tae kwon do practitioners would be wise to study some grappling moves (I realized this a long time ago and earned a black belt in ju-jutsu back in the 1980s). I am not going to cover grappling and ground

Ground fighting . Photo courtesy of Derek Alfonso.

Figure 7-12

fighting here; however, refer to the bibliography for some excellent resources. Just remember that books and videos cannot take the place of a competent instructor.

In chapter four, I listed the groin as a primary target area. And in cases where you are being harassed by a sane and sober jerk, a kick or knee to the groin will surely get him to leave you alone. But if the assailant is drunk or on drugs, that groin technique will have little to no effect (he'll be sore tomorrow, but he might get more violent with you today). And since most men have been conditioned to protect the groin, he will likely be looking for and can easily grab your kick (Figure 7-12). I suggest targeting the kneecap with your kicks and the eyes with your hands in an actual violent street confrontation.

The "Mock-Fearful" Ready Posture

As I have previously said, you don't want to portray anything but compliance until you absolutely must fight. You must appear non-

Figure 7-13

Figure 7-14

Figure 7-15

threatening while maintaining a ready posture (Figure 7-13). This is a great way to lure the perp into thinking you won't give him any trouble. Your hands are up in a mock show of fear (sometimes I call this the "weenie" posture) while you say something like, "Please let's talk about this. Don't hurt me." In reality your hands are up and prepared to block and counterstrike (Figure 7-14 to 7-15).

Light, Medium, and Hard Responses

My original instructor, Allen R. Steen, used to say that there are three levels of response in a street fight. We used the terms "light, medium, and hard."

You can probably figure out what light means. In many cases you don't really want or need to injure someone. Maybe it's your drunken uncle wanting to see some of that "kurotty." Perhaps it's the next-door neighbor who just lost his temper over your dog digging under the fence. You need to protect yourself, but you don't want to put someone in the hospital. This is the lowest response level.

A medium response is for the bully that won't leave you alone or for an obnoxious drunk in the bar. Perhaps you want to teach him a lesson, but you don't want him to have to take an ambulance ride to the emergency room—not if you can help it, that is.

The hard response is for the rapist, the violent mugger, and the crazed drug addict. He intends on hurting you, and you must protect yourself decisively.

The hardest part about this is figuring out when to use what level. I wish there were a way to know. But, as we have already discussed, you just have to use your intuition. Think about the legal ramifications of excessive force, but also remember the old saying, "Better to be tried by twelve than carried by six."

Choke

OK, let me show you some examples of self-defense responses. In Figure 7-16, the woman has been grabbed in a front choke. Let's assume she has decided to respond with the *lightest level* of self-defense technique. She inserts one open hand in between the assailant's arms (Figure 7-17). She pivots and pushes both of her attacker's arms away from her body (Figure 7-18). She should continue to retreat, possibly even turning and running.

Figure 7-16   Figure 7-17   Figure 7-18

Next we'll look at the *medium level*. Again, the defender must make her own decision as to the severity of response. Let's say she wants to let the jerk know she means business, but she isn't ready to injure him, yet. There is a little pressure point in the base of the throat (in Chinese martial arts called "conception point 22," or in Western terminology, the sternal notch). This point is very susceptible to downward pressure with the fingertips (Figure 7-19). If he has a long reach, she may need to step forward and extend her arm (Figure 7-20). He'll back away from the pain, and she should then back away from him.

Now on to the *hardest level* of response. This is the point at which

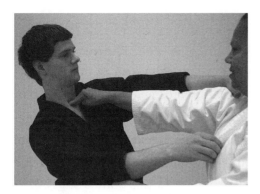

Figure 7-19   Figure 7-20

the attack is severe and she knows she has to take immediate and forceful action to defend herself.

Although I am going to show you specific techniques, it is more
important that you just start striking the predator hard and fast. It is
less important that you get every technique exactly right than it is that
you explode with violent energy

Our female victim has decided she won't be a victim for long. She
reaches directly for the perp's face with her fingers behind his ears and
her thumbs digging into his eye sockets (Figure 7-21).

As he recoils from the thumbs in his eyes, she continues by kicking
him in the kneecap. A kick to the side of the knee (Figure 7-22) causes
more damage than a straight-on strike because you can miss and still
hurt the joint by hitting a little above or below the knee.

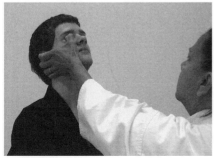

Figure 7-21   Figure 7-22

Wrist Grab

In the *light* response you will twist your hand by extending your fingers toward the weakest part of the assailant's grip (his thumb) (Figure 7-23 to 7-24). If he is stronger than you or is holding on with two hands, you may have to use both hands to escape (Figure 7-25 to 7-26).

If he is still just too strong for you to effect an escape or you sense he is setting you up for a more forceful attack, you can simply strike with your free hand—the *medium* response. At this point, I suggest an

Figure 7-23

Figure 7-24

Figure 7-25

Figure 7-26

Figure 7-27

Figure 7-28

open palm or even a backhand slap (Figure 7-27). I like open-hand strikes for self-defense more than closed fist punches because you run less risk of injuring yourself (boxers wrap their fists before a fight because punching at someone's head increases their chances of breaking their own hand). Now, take the opportunity to run.

If, however, your instincts are telling you this is a violent confrontation and you must respond at the *hardest* level, kick out to his knee (Figure 7-28). Note the raised block to the head to protect against the attacker's strike.

Rear Choke

For this particular attack I'm going to skip the *light* response for the simple fact that if someone is choking you from behind, they mean you harm, and you must protect yourself by inflicting some pain.

Pull down on the front arm (Figure 7-29), and try to tuck your chin into the bend of the attacker's elbow (Figure 7-30). This relieves the pressure on your throat momentarily. Now, drive your elbow into the solar plexus (Figure 7-31), or drop your hammer fist into the groin area (Figure 7-32). Believe it or not, this is the *medium* response because we are not causing severe injury at this point.

Figure 7-29   Figure 7-30   Figure 7-31

If you do have to cause injury (*hard* response) because the attack is particularly violent, the initial response is the same, but you now turn into the predator and drive your open hand into the throat (Figure 7-33) and your thumbs into the eyes (Figure 7-34).

Figure 7-32   Figure 7-33   Figure 7-34

The Mind-Set of the Attacker

The last thing I'll address is the bad guy's mind-set. He probably has a poor self-image and often feels powerless. A lot of people are in this predicament and go on to improve their lot in life. But some let out their frustrations by bullying others. Some turn to alcohol or drugs, and that just makes them more miserable and desperate. In extreme cases, they take a gun and go into a crowded classroom or a busy mall. Should we feel sorry for them? Yes. Should we let them take advantage of us or of others? No.

The martial arts of American karate and tae kwon do not only teach us to deal with the powerless and frustrated criminals but also help us to overcome our own feelings of frustration and fear of the unknown.

Keep training and, as the sergeant on the television show *Hill Street Blues* used to say, "Be careful out there!"

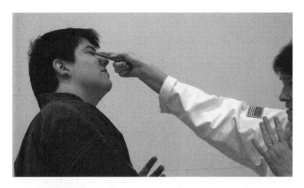 

OTHER WEAPONS: Other self-defense weapons are things like a pen or pencil or even your car keys. Targets for these weapons that you probably carry in your purse or pockets are soft areas like the throat or eyes.

Your Victim Potential

Where and how you live has a lot to do with your victim potential. Take this quiz to see where you fall on the scale. Every "yes" answer puts you closer to potential victim status.

   You live in a city with a population of more than 200,000.

   You are a teenager.

   You are female.

   You are a senior citizen.

   You are a minority race.

   You work in an occupation dealing with money and the general
     public.

   You have a quick temper.

   You abuse alcohol or drugs.

   You hitchhike or pick up hitchhikers.

   You have locked yourself out of your car more than twice.

   You wear expensive jewelry or watches.

   You often forget to lock your house when you leave.

   You wake up in the morning and realize you didn't lock your house
     for the night.

Your front door doesn't have a peephole.

If you are female, you will go out on a date with someone you barely know.

If you are male, you will get into an occasional disagreement with someone you barely know.

You wear your convention badge while outside the convention meeting place.

You will use an outdoor ATM.

You own a handgun "just for protection" but have little or no practice with it.

You often misplace your keys or your purse.

Your family doesn't have emergency code words.

You often find yourself operating on "auto-pilot," not really paying attention to your surroundings.

> *You are no more armed because you are wearing a pistol than you are a musician because you own a guitar.*
> —Jeff Cooper

Questions from Chapter Seven

■ The PRE of PRE-fight stands for _____.

■ In the majority of sexual assault cases, the attacker had been drinking. True or false?

■ Most home burglaries are crimes of opportunity. True or false?

■ If you allow yourself to be taken to a secondary crime scene, your chances of survival go way down. True or false?

■ Even black belts can "freeze" under adrenal stress. True or false?

■ You can legally punch out someone bigger than you if he calls you a dirty name. True or false?

Glossary

The Language of American Karate and Tae Kwon Do

I thought about putting a typical glossary at the back of this book, but there are many of them floating around out there, both in print and online. So I am just going to list some of the typical terms—Japanese, Korean, and English—that you are likely to hear in a classroom in this country.

Atemi. The Japanese method of striking the weak areas of an opponent's body.

Basics. The fundamental techniques—the first things you learn in class and the motions that intermediate and advanced students are supposed to have mastered.

Bo. Literally means "wood." Many karate schools use the term to refer to a five- to six-foot-long wooden staff.

Bokken. A wooden representation of a Katana, a Japanese samurai sword ("bo" is wood, and "ken" is sword).

Breakfall. A method of falling to prevent injury by rolling slightly and slapping out with a flat hand on the floor mainly to keep from hitting your head or back on the hard ground.

Broken rhythm. Not moving in a predictable, continuous pattern, a deliberate interruption of your movement to throw an opponent off guard.

Center line. An imaginary line running down the center of your body. Many targets are located on this line.

Center of gravity. Your balance is centered through your hips. This is an important point to remember when kicking or even punching. Sometimes referred to by the Japanese term, *hara*.

Centering. A teacher might tell you to stay "centered," to not be distracted by outside concerns or stresses while in class. To be "focused" means much the same thing.

Control. Refers to the ability to position your techniques in such a way that they won't actually smash into your partner's body in class. "Use more control" is frequently said to students who get overexcited in sparring matches.

Counterattack. This means to strike back at an opponent immediately after you block, parry, or avoid his initial attack against you.

Dojo. The Japanese word for the school (literally "place of the way," if you remember). I know a lot of Korean stylists who use this word instead of dojang, the actual Korean term.

Dragon. A lot of karate and tae kwon do schools like to put a picture of this mythical beast on their walls or T-shirts. It is actually one of the five animals of kung fu; the others are the snake, leopard, tiger, and crane.

Economy of motion. Basically, not making a lot of extra and unneeded movements. You should punch, kick, and block with fast and direct technique. "Efficiency of motion" is another way of saying it.

Extreme martial arts. A modern description of gymnastic moves mixed in with more traditional martial arts techniques. You'll see back flips, handstands, music, twirling weapons, etc., in what is called XMA competition.

Feint. Faking a move as a decoy to the actual technique with which you plan to score or strike.

Fighting stance. Most martial artists fight from a balance that is a little longer than a formal back stance but not as long as a forward stance.

This enables you to dance around and kick without too much shifting of your weight. The fighting stance can be "open," that is, you are both facing the same direction, or "closed," in which you are both facing opposite directions.

Footwork. How you move your feet when fighting or doing self-defense. This can be the difference between a successful technique and a spill onto the pavement.

Full-contact. Fighting without trying to "pull" or control your punches and kicks. In reality, this isn't actually all-out, to-the-death stuff. There are rules even in full-contact bouts.

Gi. The training uniform, another Japanese term that almost all Americans use whether their arts are from Japanese or Korean backgrounds. *Tobak* is the Korean uniform with a pullover top.

Ground fighting. What you are supposed to do when you are tackled or fall to the floor. Many times a karate or tae kwon do practitioner is at a disadvantage if this happens. That's why wise teachers will mix in some ground fighting in their training.

Hajime. Japanese term meaning "begin." You might hear this in a tournament from a karate referee starting a match or giving you the command to begin your form.

Hombu. Japanese term for the official headquarters of a school or system.

Jamming. Snuffing or smothering an opponent's technique before she can to complete it against you, also called "short-circuiting."

Kata. Japanese word for the training patterns you learn and practice. Most American tournaments have kata divisions for all competitors, even if they come from tae kwon do schools. By the way, the Korean translation of the same Asian character is *hyung*.

Kiai. Japanese term for the loud shout (literally "spirit shout") you are supposed to yell out when breaking boards or emphasizing a strike against an opponent. Although the Korean equivalent is "kiap," most Americans use the Japanese pronunciation. And by the way, you don't actually yell, "KEE-AYE." It's more like "AYE-YA" or, in some Japanese schools, "OS!"

Kimchi. If your teacher is Korean or trained with Koreans, then she has probably eaten this traditional pickled vegetable. Be careful, it can be hotter than jalapeños.

Kyu. The ranks below black belt in Japanese martial arts. The Korean term is gup ranks.

Linear motion. A technique delivered in a straight line. The shortest distance between two points is a straight line.

Lock. A technique that immobilizes some part of an opponent's body. You can do wrist locks, arm locks, even leg locks.

Makiwara. A striking pad usually mounted on the wall where students may beat their knuckles bloody red. My old school had a burlap one, but the modern makiwara pads are usually dense foam rubber.

Mixed martial arts. A modern approach where pretty much "anything goes." The opponents mix in techniques from striking and grappling systems to gain an advantage.

Mushin. A Buddhist concept of not allowing yourself to be distracted by outside influences. Literally means "no mind." To the samurai, mushin meant they were in a state of mind so as not to be afraid of death.

Ninja. Literally, "the stealers in," a popular costume at Halloween and Christmas parties at the karate school.

Nunchaku. It is pronounced "noon-cha-ku," not "num-chucks." Developed in Okinawa and, of course, forever popularized by Bruce Lee and other martial arts film actors.

Sanchin. Deep breathing exercises used mostly in Okinawan systems to tense and train the abdominal muscles.

Sensei. Usually thought of as meaning "teacher." Another word that, while it is Japanese, is uttered by lots of Korean-based martial artists, probably because that's what they say in all those the movies.

Takedown. Putting your opponent down on the ground. Usually refers to a sweep of the other guy's legs rather than a throw where you lift him into the air and toss him.

Tanto. A Japanese knife ranging in length from eight to fifteen inches, usually carried by the samurai in addition to their long swords. In modern day schools, a wooden *tanto* is often used for knife defense classes instead of a rubber facsimile because it hurts more if it strikes and thus makes for more serious training.

Thrust kick. Refers to a kick that isn't snapped immediately back to the starting position but instead thrusts out and through the target. Usually used as a defensive kick against a charging opponent and also is a better kick for breaking boards.

Triangulation point. A point on the ground that forms an imaginary triangle when combined with an opponent's foot positions. This is the direction where his balance will be weakest and by pushing (or pulling) him toward these points, you can make him fall.

Uke. In Japanese it literally means the "receiver," that is, the person upon whom the technique is applied. It is pronounced "oo-kay." "Tori," by the way, is the person doing the technique.

X-block. Any block in which the arms or wrists are crossed. This adds power to a single arm block and makes for an easy grab of an opponent's punch or kick.

Endnotes

Introduction

1. You'll see tae kwon do written as three words, two words (taekwon-do), and lately as one word. I still use the original English transcription with three words. Also, I will not capitalize karate and tae kwon do because I consider these terms "generic" rather than indicating a specific style like Nam Seo Kwan.

2. Donn F. Draeger, *Modern Bujutsu and Budo,* (New York: Weatherhill, 1974).

3. John Corcoran and John Graden, *The Ultimate Martial Arts Q and A Book,* (New York: Contemporary Books, 2001).

Chapter One: History

1. Takao Nakaya, *Karate-Do, History and Philosophy,* (Carrollton, TX: JSS Publishing, 1986). See also H. Neill McFarland, *Daruma—The Founder of Zen in Japanese and Popular Culture,* (Tokyo: Kodansha International, 1987).

2. Some Japanese language experts point out that the word "kara" has a larger meaning than just "empty"—it can also indicate empty as in a "blank canvas" or "unlimited potential." And none other than Chogi Motobu said that the philosophical implication of "empty" was more "forward-looking" than the old word conjuring up historical references to old China.

3. Donn F. Draeger and Robert W. Smith, *Asian Fighting Arts,* (Tokyo: Kodansha International, 1980).

4. While the samurai did practice some empty-hand techniques, in reality they used their swords as their primary weapon. Weaponless

fighting was never a large part of the classical *Bugei* (warriors).

5. Tang Soo Do uses the same written characters as karate-do, which was originally also translated as "way of the China hand." In essence, Tang Soo Do was "Korean karate."

6. For more information on the Nam Seo Kwan system curriculum, go to www.akato.org.

Chapter Two: Philosophy

1. As I mentioned in chapter one, karate and tae kwon do cannot even trace their history to the samurai anyway.

2. Draeger, *Modern Bujutsu and Budo*.

3. Mushin doesn't mean you are "mind-less." Actually, it means the opposite—that you are able to see and comprehend more clearly, without distractions. Your judgment is not clouded with preconceptions.

4. Draeger, *Modern Bujutsu and Budo*.

Chapter Three: Procedures

1. Dave Lowry, *In the Dojo*, (Boston: Weatherhill, 2006).

2. Kano first awarded black belts as a symbol of rank in 1886. At that time there were just two colors: white for juniors and black for seniors. The addition of other colors like green and brown can probably be attributed to Mikonosuke Kawaishi, who later took judo to Europe.

3. A more literal translation is the "place of the way." Remember that "do" means "way."

4. Those who know a few Japanese and Korean terms will note that the rank just below black belt is called a first kyu (or gup in Korean)—Ikyu. But the first black belt is not an "I" or "Ichi" dan but a "sho" dan. Why is this? "Sho" more literally means beginner. So a shodan (or chodan in Korean) isn't merely a first degree black belt, he or she is a beginner black belt.

5. Lowry, *In the Dojo*.

6. John Corcoran, *The Martial Arts Sourcebook*, (New York: Harper Collins Publishing, 1994).

Chapter Four: Physical Aspects

1. Yes, research shows that you can increase your general health levels by being active for just a few minutes at a time (like walking up the stairs at work) as long as you do that several times a day every day, but I am talking about an increase in your cardiovascular endurance levels, and that means getting your heart pumping hard for those fifteen minutes.

Chapter Five: Training Patterns

1. Michael Rosenbaum, *Kata and the Transmission of Knowledge*, (Boston: YMAA Publishing, 2004).
2. I am going to use the Japanese term *kata* here instead of the Korean terms *hyung, tul,* or *poomse* because most American stylists know and use it almost exclusively.

Chapter Six: Sparring

1. Masatoshi Nakayama, *Fighting Arts International.* Issue 46.
2. Benny Urquidez, *Training and Fighting Skills*, (Hollywood, CA: Unique Publications, 1980).

Chapter Seven: Self-Defense

1. Gavin de Becker, *The Gift of Fear*, (New York: Dell Publishing, 1997).
2. Randall Hassell, *Karate: Zen, Pen, and Sword*, (Empire Books, 2006).
3. Payton Quinn, *Real Fighting*, (Boulder, CO: Paladin Press, 1996).
4. John Perkins, Al Ridenhour, and Matt Kovsky, *Attack Proof: The Ultimate Guide to Personal Protection*, (Champaign, IL: Human Kinetics, 2000).
5. Jeff Cooper, *Principles of Personal Defense*, (Boulder, CO: Paladin Press, 1972).

Arakaki, Kiyoshi. *The Secrets of Okinawan Karate.* Tokyo: Kodansha International, 2000.

Ashirhara, Hideyuki. *Fighting Karate.* Tokyo: Kodansha Ltd., 1985.

Beasley, Jerry. *The Development of American Karate.* Greenville, NC: Bemjo Martial Arts Library, 1983.

Borkowshi, Cezar, and Marion Manzo. *The Complete Idiot's Guide to the Martial Arts.* Upper Saddle River, NJ: Prentice Hall, 1999.

Bowerbank, Andrew. *Spirit of the Sensei: A Study of Japanese Martial Arts.* Toronto: Morris Marketing, 1998.

Burgar, Bill. *Five Years, One Kata.* U.K.: Martial Arts Publishing Ltd., 2003.

Choi, Hong Hi. *Taekwon-Do, The Art of Self-Defense.* Seoul: Hwasong Publishing, 1965.

Clark, Rick. *75 Down Blocks: Refining Karate Technique.* Boston: Tuttle Publishing, 2003.

Clayton, Bruce. *Shotokan's Secret: The Hidden Truth Behind Karate's Fighting Origins.* California: Ohara Publications, 2005.

Cooper, Jeff. *Principles of Personal Defense.* Boulder, CO: Paladin Press, 1972.

Corcoran, John. *The Martial Arts Sourcebook.* New York: Harper Collins Publishing, 1994.

Corcoran, John and Emil Farkas. *Martial Arts: Traditions, History and People.* New York: Gallery Books, 1983.

Corcoran, John, and John Graden. *The Ultimate Martial Arts Q and A Book.* New York: Contemporary Books, 2001.

de Becker, Gavin. *The Gift of Fear.* New York: Dell Publishing, 1997.

Dillman, George. *Kyusho Jitsu: The Dillman Method of Pressure Point Fighting.* Reading, PA: George Dillman Karate International, 1992.

Draeger, Donn F. *Modern Bujutsu and Budo.* New York: Weatherhill, 1974.

Draeger, Donn F., and Robert W. Smith. *Asian Fighting Arts.* Toyko: Kodansha International, 1980.

Finn, Michael. *Martial Arts: A Complete Illustrated History.* New York: The Overlook Press, 1988.

Hassell, Randall. *Karate: Zen, Pen, and Sword.* Empire Books, 2006.

Kee, Hwang. *Tang Soo Do Soo Bahk Do.* Springfield, NJ: Sung Moon Sa, 1978.

Kurz, Thomas. *Stretching Scientifically: A Guide to Flexibility Training.* Island Pond, VT: Stadion Publishing, 1994.

Lowry, Dave. *In the Dojo.* Boston: Weatherhill, 2006.

Lowry, Dave. *Sword and Brush.* Boston: Shambhala Publications, 1995.

Martinez, Javier. *Isshinryu: Naihanchi Kata Secrets Revealed.* San Juan, PR: Martinez Publisher, 1999.

McFarland, H. Neill. *Daruma: The Founder of Zen in Japanese and Popular Culture.* Toyko: Kodansha International, 1987.

Morgan, Forrest E. *Living the Martial Way.* Fort Lee, NJ: Barricade Books, 1992.

Morris, Vince, and Aidan Trimble. *Karate Kata and Applications.* London: Random Century, 1990.

Nakaya, Takao. *Karate-Do, History and Philosophy.* Carrollton, TX: JSS Publishing, 1983.

Perkins, John, Al Ridenhour, and Matt Kovsky. *Attack Proof: The Ultimate Guide to Personal Protection.* Champaign, IL: Human Kinetics, 2000.

Quinn, Payton. *Real Fighting.* Boulder, CO: Paladin Press, 1996.

Rhee, Jhoon. *Bruce Lee and I.* Fairfax, VA: MVM Books, 2000.

Rosenbaum, Michael. *Kata and the Transmission of Knowledge.* Boston: YMAA Publishing, 2004.

Shapiro, Amy. *The Running Press Glossary of Martial Arts Language.* Philadelphia: Running Press, 1978.

Tedeschi, Marc. *Essential Anatomy for Healing and the Martial Arts.* New York: Weatherhill, 2000.

Umezawa, Rui. *The Empty Hand: A Karate Workbook.* New York: Weatherhill, 1998.

Urquidez, Benny. *Training and Fighting Skills.* Hollywood, CA: Unique Publications, 1980.

Wallace, Bill and Charles Roy Schroeder. *Karate Basic Concepts and Skills.* Philippines: Addison-Wesley, 1976.

Photo Credits

Cover images by C. David Edmonson

pg vi　　Photo by Lyman Roark

pg xvii　Photo by C. David Edmonson

pg 12　　Courtesy of Mark Williams

pg 12　　Courtesy of Paul Tarrant

pg 13　　Courtesy of Ed Parker Jr.

pg 14　　Courtesy of J. Pat Burleson

pg 16　　Courtesy of Skipper Mullins

pg 18　　Courtesy of Roy Kurban

pg 27　　Courtesy of Top Kick Productions

pg 30　　Courtesy of Mike Allen and Joe Lewis

pg 43　　Courtesy of the Kick Start Foundation

pg 53　　Courtesy of Jhoon Rhee

pg 57　　Courtesy of Mike Allen and Joe Lewis

pg 74　　Courtesy of Pat Burleson

pg 76　　Courtesy of Rob Vanellei

pg 79　　Courtesy of Troy Dorsey

pg 89　　Courtesy of the Cooper Institute

pg 116　Courtesy of Linda Denley

pg 129　Courtesy of John Chung

pg 156　Courtesy of Derek Alfonso

pg 157　Courtesy of the World Combat League

pg 179　Courtesy of Derek Alfonso

All illustrations by Keith Yates. Other photos were taken
by Keith Yates or his students. Special thanks to Kathy Rhine
for not only photography but for her editing assistance.

Photo Models

Halleh Bahramnejad	Thomas Merhout
Derek Baird	Ysabel Merhout
Sheryl Baird	Randy Miller
Benjamin Baker	Drake Pledger
Aaron Barnett	Mike Proctor
Alex Brown	Kathy Rhine
Jill Boudreaux	Elizabeth Rogan
Hunter Brooks	Caleb Skipper
Austin Brown	Tony Tempesta
David Buford	Alton Thibodeaux
Kelly Cox	Tommy Vaughn
Miles Crietzberg	Jennifer Vilches
Velmore Estillore	Rob Whapham
Caroline Goodspeed	Tabatha Whapham
Garrett Griffith	Geoff White
Terry Heronime	Faith Yates
Katie Huffner	Rodney Yates
Merrill Matthews	Warren Vincent